Spirituality of Struggle

Andrew Mayes trained for the priesthood at King's College London – where he was awarded a First in Theology – and at St Stephen's House, Oxford. During a year at the Armenian Seminary, Jerusalem, he studied Orthodox spirituality, sponsored by the Philip Usher Memorial Scholarship. Subsequently, he studied Catholic spirituality at Heythrop College, London, and the Evangelical tradition at the Nazarene Theological College, Manchester. He was awarded an MA in Theology – with distinction – by Manchester University in 1997. He has served in parishes in London, Essex, Birmingham and Saltdean. He is currently the Bishop's Officer for Continuing Ministerial Education in the Diocese of Chichester, and parish priest of Ovingdean. He is a co-author of a catechetical programme, *Following Jesus*, and a contributor to a symposium on the Oriental Orthodox Churches, *Light from the East*. His *Celebrating the Christian Centuries*, a course on spirituality, was published by SPCK in 1999.

To Verity, Simon, Lucy, Adam and
the next generation of strugglers

Spirituality of Struggle

Pathways to Growth

Andrew D. Mayes

First published in Great Britain in 2002 by
SPCK, Holy Trinity Church, Marylebone Road,
London NW1 4DU

British Library Cataloguing-in-Publication Data

A catalogue record for this book is available from the
British Library

ISBN 0281–05420–7

Typeset by FiSH Books, London WC1
Printed in Great Britain by Omnia Books, Glasgow

Contents

Introduction

Today increasing numbers of people struggle as they try
to find a faith that is relevant to their lives and a
meaningful relationship with the divine. Those outside
the Christian community feel hesitant to enter it,
because they do not feel they have attained a sufficient
level of faith. Those inside the Church who struggle
sometimes feel awkward or self-conscious because they
do not share the confident, strong faith of those around
them. This book offers encouragement and hope to
people who struggle in their spiritual journey. It declares
that struggles can be the very way we find God and
work out a mature and reflective faith. They open up a
route to spirituality, prayer and discovery of God; they
can become pathways to growth.

In fact, the Bible includes many stories of people who
struggle. These characters are real flesh-and-blood
people. They become archetypes, basic figures who reach
out through the centuries to our own lives. The Bible tells
us their stories – almost primordial tales of struggles
which face people in every age. In the Old Testament,
characters are often set forth as exemplars, as types and
images which mirror the experience of the emerging
people of God. They seem to stand for the nation, the
people God is calling into being. In their conflicts, we
recognize our own search for identity and vocation. In
the New Testament, stories of struggling individuals are
included because they represent something of what
Christians face: they stand for us. In fact the theme of

'struggling with God' appears as a key which can unlock the Bible for today's readers.

Although twenty-first-century characteristics mark our own spiritual struggles, and they reflect the pressures of our time, in many ways the struggles we face are common to all ages. People have been here before us. In this book we will explore these timeless struggles. It is intended both as a tool for personal study and as a resource for groups.

- Each chapter will look at one type of struggle, and one personality in the Bible who shows us a possible response.
- There will be scripture passages focusing the issues.
- There will also be reference in most chapters to a spirituality writer who is reflecting on these themes. With their help, we will sketch out a spirituality – a way of praying or thinking through each type of spiritual conflict.
- There will be questions to stimulate individual reflection or group discussion.
- There will be a choice of two 'Prayer Exercises' which can serve as a useful conclusion to any group session.

The Bible opens with a man and a woman finding themselves in the midst of a bitter struggle. The figures of Adam and Eve in the garden of Eden represent humanity's quest in every age – our capacity to discover God as Creator and Friend, and also our stubborn desire to go our own way. But above all, they hold out to the reader a vision of what we are called to – enjoying communion with God who alone makes sense of our lives. In this book, while we grapple with barriers and issues that come across our path, we will not lose sight of this fundamental invitation: to walk with God in the cool of the day.

Chapter 1

Struggling with identity

The most fundamental and crucial questions which face each person are 'Who am I?' and 'How can I be sure that God loves me?' These are questions raised by the figure of Jacob in the book of Genesis, the book of beginnings, in the Bible. The story of Jacob's struggle related in Genesis 32.22–31 has touched the hearts and minds of people from time immemorial because it echoes the experience of man in every age. It will introduce for us various themes that we will be exploring in this book. Like the story of Adam and Eve, it can be read as a parable that deals with basic issues of life itself. It is an archetypal tale, for it represents the struggle of Everyman.

It is the struggle of Man with God. Jacob wrestled and fought with a Stranger, an unknown figure. We never learn his name but, describing his encounter later, Jacob said: 'I have seen God face to face.' It was indeed a divine–human combat.

Jacob is truly a representative figure in this story. First, he stands for the Jewish people. He is given the name 'Israel', with an explanation that this means 'one who struggles with God'. The very name which comes to denote the chosen people affirms the place of struggling with God. Jacob, son of Isaac and grandson of Abraham, is a 'patriarch', a founding father of the nation. He personifies the people of Israel. As the Old Testament scholar Gerhard von Rad writes about this story: 'it contains experiences of faith that extend from

the most ancient period down to the time of the
narrator; there is charged to it something of the result of
the entire divine history into which Israel was
drawn...as it is now related it is clearly transparent as
a type of that which Israel experienced from time to time
with God. Israel has here presented its entire history
with God almost prophetically as such a struggle until
the breaking of the day'.[1] But the figure of Jacob in this
tale also represents the Christian. Paul calls the Church
'the new Israel', and insists that we are the children and
offspring of Abraham. So we can truly see ourselves in
Jacob and recognize our struggles in his.

The ancient story of Genesis 32 contains seven
symbolic elements that we will explore. In language
which is evocative, enigmatic and elusive, it speaks
across the centuries to our own experience.

The journey: 'The same night he arose'

The life of Jacob depicted in Genesis is the story of a
man in search of his identity. Jacob found it very hard to
accept that God loved him, for himself as an individual,
and that God wanted him for himself. The struggle at
the Jabbok river was the culmination of a life of trying
to come to terms with the reality of God.

In a sense the journey begins when Jacob emerges
from Rebekah his mother's womb, clutching the heel of
his elder twin born seconds before him (Genesis 25.26).
From his first moment Jacob grows up in the shadow of
Esau. He seems to be continually overshadowed by Esau
who is his father's favourite. In an age when honour and
privilege went to the first-born son, Jacob feels
intimidated and suffers some kind of inferiority
complex. His life is marked by fierce rivalry and
competition. He comes to see himself as a second best
and resorts to deception and deviousness to get the

upper hand. Twice Jacob tricks his brother. He gets him to sell his birthright, his privileges as the elder son, for a single meal (25.29–33). Later when his blind father Isaac wishes to solemnly impart his blessing and the guarantee of inheritance, Jacob pretends to be Esau. Jacob cannot accept that God has plans for his own life, so he tries to advance himself. Lacking faith and trust in God, Jacob takes a path of stubborn self-reliance. But after robbing Esau of his rightful blessing, Jacob must flee to escape his brother's vengeance. This journey represents Jacob's quest for identity, his personal search to make something of his life in his own right.

He travels hundreds of miles from the south of Canaan to Haran in the far north (near today's Turkish/Syrian border). He settles with distant relatives and is shamefully mistreated by his uncle Laban who exacts 20 years' service from him in return for the promise of his daughter Rachel in marriage. This is a time of painful exile for Jacob, far from his parents' home. It is his turn to be duped and cheated by others. But after Rachel bears him the gift of a son, Jacob knows it is time to return home. He is pursued by angry Laban who cannot let go of his daughters. A long and tiresome trek south brings Jacob into the area where he will expect to encounter his estranged brother Esau. Jacob is eaten up with anxiety and fear as he realizes he must pass into Esau's territory. He devises a plan to appease Esau with a substantial gift. His past is catching up with him once again, and his future stretches ahead of him: but first he must cross the waters of the Jabbok. Jacob arrives at the Jabbok weary and conscious of his own failings and fears. He has manipulated others, and suffered abuse himself. He is vulnerable – and also ready for an encounter with God.

We can identify with Jacob in several ways. In our life's journey we also get bruised and disenchanted with others. God gives us, like Jacob, the freedom and the space to make our own mistakes. God's gift of free will allows us to shape our own destiny and make our own choices. Like Jacob, we can find it hard to believe God is really interested in our own life. The vital thing is that we allow our pains and fears and hurts to pass over into an encounter with God.

In today's technological and computerized world, which often fosters a sense of anonymity and impersonality, we need to rediscover our true worth in God's eyes. Like Jacob, we can lose perspective on our true dignity. We need to learn, as he was to learn at the Jabbok river, that our real value comes not from what others might say about us, but from what God has to say about us.

Jacob kept moving in his journey and when he came face to face with God, he brought with him all his insecurities. He did not seek to evade God. At times in our own journey, we too may feel insignificant, insecure. Yet God is waiting for us in the waters. He is beckoning us to move into them, just as we are.

Reaching the frontier: 'He crossed the ford of the Jabbok'

The Jabbok ford is close to the Jordan, and forms part of the boundary of Canaan, the promised land. It represents a threshold into the future, the possibility of a new beginning. In more than one sense it represents a limit. Jacob has reached the limit of his own resources. He has grasped and schemed and tried by his own cleverness to gain success. Now he stands on the brink of discovering that God longs for him. The Jabbok represents a frontier – the line that marks the edge of his capabilities also marks the start, the fringes of the promised land, the land of freedom.

Jacob could have viewed the Jabbok in more negative terms. It could have become for him a barrier – a
place to halt and go no further. But he realizes that the
river, though a place of potential danger, is essentially
a ford, a crossing-over place, a way to get from one
territory to another. It represents for us a place of transition, where God calls us courageously to face new
possibilities. Encounter with God can be a risky business. But it can also enable us in our life to cross
boundaries – by letting go of the past, we can embrace
a new future.

From Jacob's vantage point, he could also see far
ahead. Before him lay the great rift valley of the
Jordan, and beyond it, through the mists rising from
the Dead Sea, he could make out in the distance the
first craggy mountains of Canaan, the land of promise.
To come to a true sense of our identity, we sometimes
need to look away from our ourselves and recapture a
sense of the otherness of God. Things start to take on
a new perspective when we place ourselves in the
larger picture. Too often, we are the centre of our own
universe. Like Jacob, we need to see horizons once
again, which beckon us to move beyond ourselves and
which remind us that God is there, in our future.

Before Jacob stretched a vast panorama, a vista
stretching many miles. It calls to mind lines from
Frederick Faber's great hymn:

> There's a wideness in God's mercy like the wideness of
>   the sea . . .
> For the love of God is broader than the measures of
>   man's mind . . .
> But we make His love too narrow by false limits of our
>   own
> And we magnify His strictness with a zeal He will not
>   own.

Passing through the waters: 'across the stream'

Jacob's struggle with God takes place in the depths of the river Jabbok, the place where travellers pass over. There is a splashing and scrambling amidst the swirling currents. The account has echoes of the opening verses of Genesis: 'The earth was without form and void, and darkness was upon the face of the deep; and the Spirit of God was moving over the face of the waters.' The Bible opens with a picture of primordial chaos in the waters. The waters are the place where God begins his creation. Even more significantly, to the readers of Genesis, the waters flowing through the Jabbok evoke of the memory of the Exodus. The waters have become a powerful symbol of liberation for the people of Israel, recalled each Passover. Moses led his people through the Red Sea to freedom, escaping the slavery and oppression of Egypt, and the waters flooded back and drowned the enemy pursuing them.

For Christian readers, the waters of the Jabbok recall the experience of baptism. For Christians, the waters of baptism are a place of death and resurrection effecting a dying to self, a dying to the old way of life. Our rising from the water marks a sharing in Christ's resurrection and in the newness of life that Christ brings. This is the Christian 'passover', the passing from death to new life.

Though baptism is a once and for all event, we have to return to the waters, as we do in worship each Easter. We have to make our own, again and again, the victory of baptism. We have to go back to the waters and struggle and fight again and again as we seek to break through to new triumphs in Christian journey. For Christians, all spirituality is *paschal* – that is, marked by the Easter mystery of death and resurrection. Augustine said: 'We are an Easter people and Alleluia is our song.'

In Chapter 9 we will examine more closely the significance of baptism for daily living. For the moment, let us allow this image of Jacob grappling with God in the splashing waters to speak to us powerfully of our daily struggle to enter in to all that baptism signifies. All our life we will be struggling in the waters to make a reality of this dying to sin and selfishness, and rising to newness of life. All our life God will be calling us to enter more fully into the Easter mystery, to appropriate it and make it our own ever more deeply. It is better not to hover on the brink of the river and avoid this struggle. God invites us to take the plunge, to step into the waters and to meet him face to face. The swirling waters represent the place of struggling with God, but it is here that liberation and re-creation will be experienced.

Alone with God: 'Jacob was left alone'

We must have space in our prayers for solitude if we are to encounter God deeply. For Jacob this meant a letting go, for the moment, of attachments to people and possessions. He was prepared to part from family and to stand alone.

Solitude is an essential element in a spirituality of struggle. We must make time and find a place where we can be real with God. The Desert Fathers of the fourth century went out into the wilderness to seek God. They found the desert to be a place of truth. It was like entering a state of spiritual nakedness before God, where masks drop off and there is no place to hide.

To be alone with God is not easy. It is demanding and it is risky. Jacob did not know what to expect but he sensed he had to cross the ford entirely alone. If we are to meet with God, we must be ready to stop hiding behind fine-sounding prayers and holy books. All these 'props' can become barriers to God, ways of evading a direct encounter with God. Rather we need the courage to come before God and honestly expose to him our heart's longings and fears. To enter solitude is to come to a place of vulnerability and utter openness to God. As Henri Nouwen put it:

> Solitude is thus the place of purification and transformation, the place of the great struggle and the great encounter. Solitude...is the place where Christ remodels us in his own image and frees us from the victimizing compulsions of the world. Solitude is the place of salvation.[2]

Solitude is, above all, the place where we can learn to receive from God. All his life, Jacob was used to making it on his own, and striving by his own schemes to get his way with God. In his experience of solitude at the Jabbok, Jacob would discover that blessing comes from God, not by his own efforts, but by clinging to God in the silence. This is a real problem for Christians today, taught by the world to get results by working hard, by achieving. Targets of productivity are set, and pressures mount, for rewards are dependent on what we can do. But this is a timeless issue too: was not the major debate of the Reformation in the sixteenth century precisely over this issue – whether we reach God through our own works or through God's gift of grace?

The problem is, we are not very good at receiving from God. We would rather *do* something. Solitude teaches us the hard lesson – give up trying to achieve all the time. Start receiving.

Entering the darkness: 'and a man wrestled with him until the breaking of the day'

Jacob's struggle with the divine Stranger takes place in the darkness. It is night. It was John of the Cross who coined the phrase 'the dark night of the soul'. This sixteenth-century Spanish mystic gave three reasons for using this image to describe aspects of the spiritual journey. First, says John, in the dark we cannot actually see. In the deeper reaches of prayer, we need to shut down our five senses because they hold us captive in a state of attachment to the material world and activate our self-seeking appetites. Second, in the dark we cannot easily make out obstacles or turnings along the path, so we must move forward in trust. 'We walk by faith, not by sight.' In our relationship with God we must take the risk of moving forwards without knowing the precise route. We venture into the unknown. Third, John says, the darkness speaks of God himself as Mystery. God is not something we can box in and neatly label – God is quite beyond our best concepts and categories. But 'the dark night of the soul' is not for John a negative experience, but rather a time of growth and healing. In his great poem he writes:

> O guiding night!
> O night more lovely than the dawn!
> O night that has united
> the Lover with his beloved,
> transforming the beloved in her Lover![3]

The night, for John, and for Jacob, is a place of transformation. It represents a time when we allow God to do his work powerfully within us, reshaping and redirecting our ego, and leading us into a greater surrender to God.

Many spiritual writers in fact use the image of 'darkness' to speak of entering into the mysterious presence of God. The English fourteenth-century author of *The Cloud of Unknowing* puts it like this:

When you first begin, you find only darkness, and as it were, a cloud of unknowing. You don't know what this means except that in your will you feel a simple

steadfast intention reaching out towards God...
Reconcile yourself to wait in this darkness as long as is
necessary, but still go on longing after him whom you
love. For if you are to feel him or to see him in this life,
it must always be in this cloud, in this darkness.[4]

The experience of darkness in our spiritual life can be
bewildering, unsettling, and even threatening. But we
can see it as a time for healing and truthful encounter
with God. It is precisely in this darkness that Jacob
receives unspeakable blessing. But not before he is
wounded by God.

**The wounding: 'When the man saw that he did not prevail
against Jacob, he touched the hollow of his thigh; and
Jacob's thigh was put out of joint as he wrestled with
him... The sun rose upon him as he passed Penuel,
limping because of his thigh.'**

Jacob is brought to a point of brokenness. He had, it
seems, often been on the run – running away from Esau
and fleeing to the far north, running from Laban who
chased him from Haran, and running from God – always
avoiding facing up to God, evading opportunities to bring
to God his true feelings and failures. Now Jacob can run
no longer. His running had been symbolic both of his
desire to escape uncomfortable truths and conflicts, and of
his desire to stay in control of his life. He would go where
he wished to go, and no one would stop him.

Now he can only limp. God touches him and disables
him. He is reduced to a state of new dependence on
God himself. This wounding of Jacob represents God
finally melting his stubbornness, wilfulness and self-
centredness. For the moment, at least, he crumples up.
He loses control. God has the mastery. God paralyses
his defiant, independent ego.

In his poems and in his prose, John of the Cross speaks often of God's 'wound of love': 'You have wounded me in order to cure me, O divine hand!' The pain of the 'dark night', according to John, is the costly lowering of our 'defence mechanisms' before the living God. We have self-protective strategies that try to keep God at a safe distance – where he cannot disturb us too much! We fence ourselves off to protect ourselves from too close an involvement with God. But if we are to experience God in reality, we must allow ourselves to be vulnerable to God. Something has to give.

That 'something' is often our desire and need to remain in control, to be at the helm of our own lives, to make our own choices, to set our own agendas. But this can be the working of a 'false self' because it is denying God's grace and power. A new 'Self', where God is in control, only emerges, says John, in the crucible of prayer where we allow God to burn up our rampant egotism. To return to the image of the 'wounding', the pain we must face is the pain of 'letting go' of being in control, the cost of being stripped of our egotistical powers. It is a bereavement, a loss.

This is a real struggle for Christians and seekers today, because it seems so contrary to the spirit of the age which exalts independent success and an 'every man for himself' mentality. Yet, paradoxically, this costly path leads to fulfilment in and through God: 'For whoever would save his life will lose it; and whoever loses his life for my sake and the gospel's will save it' (Mark 8.35). The word 'save' here in Christ's words can be translated 'heal'. This fundamental dispossession hurts but it also heals, because it restores to us a sense of wholeness, as we become the people God wants us to be, utterly surrendered to him and available to him. As Peter Slattery puts it:

The abandonment of self-mastery and the taking on of a radical dependence on God will necessarily be accompanied by a sense of being undone or being annihilated, yet such an anxiety is quite ungrounded. In fact, the discovery that one can no longer find one's guarantees in oneself may indeed be a sign that progress in the life with God is finally being achieved.[5]

Jacob moves towards wholeness in God as his pride and self-centred stubbornness are wounded. But he also moves towards a new sense of identity.

A new identity: 'Then he said, "Let me go, for the day is breaking." But Jacob said, "I will not let you go, unless you bless me."'

Jacob, once so content to go his own way, now finds himself clinging to God. Jacob, who once sought by deceptive means to acquire blessing (deceiving his father Isaac), now cries out to God in a state of utter dependence.

This image of Jacob holding on tenaciously to God amid the splashing waters is a vivid picture of Christ's Beatitude: 'Blessed are the poor in spirit [those who know their need of God], for theirs is the kingdom of heaven' (Matthew 5.3). The change wrought in Jacob in his struggle with God is not that overnight he will become a righteous and gracious person. Rather it is that his pride is brought low and at last he surrenders to God.

And so Jacob receives the blessing he sought – a powerful reassurance that God loves him for himself. Even more than this, God gives him a new name: 'Your name shall no more be called Jacob, but Israel, for you have striven with God and with men, and have prevailed.'

Jacob's experience of receiving a new name is a moment of profound affirmation by God. It declares that God is interested in Jacob himself. It declares that there is a uniqueness about Jacob – that God wants him for *himself* – that God has plans for him. This new name indicates a chosenness, a sense that God has set his love on him. The new name represents the reality that God has a singular vocation in store for each person. But what is the meaning of the new name given to Jacob in the waters of the Jabbok? Formerly, Jacob's name meant 'Grasper'. The new name that will come to denote a nation and will represent the people of God means 'he who struggles with God'.

In giving Jacob this identity God recognizes the role of struggling in an evolving relationship with him. God is declaring that it is OK to struggle with him. It is part of the spiritual journey. It is not to be avoided but faced. Indeed, in embracing our struggles with God we emerge with new strength and a clearer sense of our identity. Jacob the Grasper becomes Israel, God's warrior. Christ promises to Christians of every age: 'To him who conquers, I will give...a new name' (Revelation 2.17). In our wrestling with God we too may discover a new name for ourselves, revealed by God. If we allow him, God will hold on to us as we battle with him in the waters, and affirm us as the ones he loves.

The narrative of Genesis continues: 'And Jacob lifted up his eyes and looked, and behold, Esau was coming' (Genesis 33.1). Jacob immediately must face the brother he always had feared. He experiences a wonderful reconciliation. Then he resumes his journey and passes into the promised land: 'And Jacob came safely to the city of Shechem, which is in the land of Canaan...There he erected an altar and dedicated it: "to God, the God of the one who struggles"' (Genesis 33.18, 20, RSV adapted).

Questions for Discussion or Reflection

1. What line strikes you most in the Genesis account, and in this chapter. Why?
2. What threatens our sense of identity today? What affirms us? How can we encourage each other?
3. How can we live out each day our baptismal identity as a son or daughter of God? How will this change our attitude to the challenges we face?

Prayer Exercise

Either

Read slowly and prayerfully Psalm 139.1–18. As you ponder this, surrender to God your doubts and insecurities. Waiting in the silence, prepare to receive a sense of God's enfolding and affirming love as he whispers to you 'You are my beloved son, my chosen daughter: my delight rests on you!' Then write your own short 'psalm' to celebrate your God-given uniqueness. Conclude with these lines from Charles Wesley's hymn:

> Come, O thou Traveller unknown,
> Whom still I hold, but cannot see:
> My company before is gone,
> And I am left alone with Thee;
> With Thee all night I mean to stay
> And wrestle till the break of day.
>
> I need not tell Thee who I am,
> My misery and sin declare;
> Thyself hast called me by my name,
> Look on Thy hands and read it there:
> But Who, I ask Thee, Who art Thou?
> Tell me Thy name, and tell me now...

'Tis Love, 'tis Love, Thou diedst for me!
I hear Thy whisper in my heart;
The morning breaks, the shadows flee,
Pure, universal Love Thou art:
To me, to all, thy mercies move;
Thy nature and Thy name is Love.

Or

Pour water slowly into a glass bowl as a visual reminder
to you of the font or place of your baptism. Reflect on
the new baptismal rite and its promises.

To follow Christ means dying to sin and rising to new
life with him.
Do you reject the devil and all rebellion against God?
I reject them.
Do you renounce the deceit and corruption of evil?
I renounce them.
Do you repent of the sins that separate us from God
and neighbour? *I repent of them.*
Do you turn to Christ as Saviour? *I turn to Christ.*
Do you submit to Christ as Lord? *I submit to Christ.*
Do you come to Christ, the way, the truth and the
life? *I come to Christ.*

May God, who has received you by baptism into
his church, pour upon you the riches of his grace, that
within the company of Christ's pilgrim people you
may daily be renewed by his anointing Spirit, and
come to the inheritance of the saints in glory. Amen.[6]

Notes

1. von Rad, G., *Genesis*. Old Testament Library, SCM
   Press, London, 1972, p. 320.
2. Nouwen, H. J. M., *The Way of the Heart*. Darton,
   Longman & Todd, London, 1981, p. 31.

3. Kavanaugh, K. & Rodriguez, O. (trs.), *The Collected Works of St John of the Cross*. Institute of Carmelite Studies, Washington DC, 1991.

4. Wolters, C. (tr.), *The Cloud of Unknowing*. Penguin, Harmondsworth, 1961, p. 53.

5. Slattery, P., *St John of the Cross*. Alba House, New York, 1994, p. 97.

6. *Common Worship: Initiation Services*. Church House Publishing, London, 1998.

Chapter 2

Struggling with change

We live in an age of unremitting change. In today's world we find ourselves buffeted and swept along by fast-moving currents of change and we can hardly keep up. It is difficult to keep abreast of the myriad developments – in technology, science, medicine, education. In addition to these very contemporary changes, we encounter age-old changes that have faced people in every generation: getting married, moving home, separation from loved ones, death of parents, illness, disability. Some take the form of bereavements, losses, when we have to part from familiar people and lifestyles, and face up to new circumstances and challenges. How do these changes affect our spirituality, our relationship with God? How can we encourage a creative attitude which is open to change? How can we live for today without fear of the future?

'Here below to live is to change, and to be perfect is to have changed often' wrote John Henry Newman. Change can be positive, enhancing personal development, but it can also be threatening and painful, as we are called to let go of well loved securities. How often do we hear the cry 'We don't like change here!' For as well as these external changes that take place around us, there are many personal changes that must happen within ourselves – gradual changes in perception and outlook, even revolutions within us as we face up to personal advances in understanding and knowledge. How can we discover an approach that will enable us to grow spiritually, develop our faith and not be blocked or closed to God's surprises?

We have much to learn from the story of Ruth in the Old Testament. She lived in an age of change and insecurity, the time when Judges ruled Israel. Joshua's conquest of Canaan was by no means complete, and Jewish tribes continued to fight with hostile local groups. It was a time when leadership was faltering: 'In those days there was no king in Israel; every man did what was right in his own eyes' (Judges 21.25). Naomi sought to escape this as she left her native Bethlehem behind her and went with her husband in search of food across the Jordan to the land of Moab. There her two sons took local Moabite wives Orpah and Ruth. But the next ten years brought three deaths, those of Naomi's husband and both her sons. The women are left desolate, and Naomi resolves to return to Bethlehem, bidding farewell to her daughters-in-law. She tries to send them back to their own villages, and the women are faced with agonizing choices. Orpah accepts Naomi's recommendation and returns to her place of origin, but Ruth feels impelled to journey with Naomi into an unknown land and an uncertain future. She says to Naomi: 'Where you go I will go, and where you lodge I will lodge' (Ruth 1.16).

Different ways of responding to change

Ruth struggles to come to terms with major upheaval in her life. First, she must face the loss of her husband. We do not know the circumstances of his death but he was young and it was tragic and unexpected – nothing could have prepared Ruth for this. Within her society, the loss of a husband also entails the loss of status – she is now a widow, and she is without income or security. Second, she faces the choice of remaining where she is, returning to her native village, or venturing into a strange land. Ruth displays tremendous big-heartedness and courage as she resolves to travel with Naomi across the Jordan. She shakes off any fears that seep into her mind – and she refuses to be 'sensible' and play it safe by staying put among her own people. She does not give in to the lethargy or depression which can so easily invade the newly bereaved. She firmly says 'no' to any fatalistic thinking that might whisper to her to accept her lot passively and she rejects the temptation to sit around until something better comes along. She will go with Naomi. She will face the challenge of meeting new people and entering a different culture and society, where she will be an outsider, an alien, a foreigner (see 2.6, 10). Ruth is ready to relinquish her ties, say goodbye to her former way of life, even separate from her mother and father (2.11). She is ready to break with the past and look to the future. To Naomi she is emphatic: 'Your people shall be my people, and your God my God' (2.16).

In these words, Ruth also reveals herself to be astonishingly open spiritually. She is prepared to leave familiar idols behind, and venture towards an unknown God. What sort of God will she discover in Bethlehem? She will be told about a God on the move, a pilgrim God who goes with his people in their journey from oppression to liberation. She will be told about a God who dwells in the midst of his people, leading them by a pillar of cloud by day and a pillar of fire by night. She will discover a God who opens up new futures for his people.

Ruth's open attitude to change contrasts markedly with the defensive, self-protective strategies adopted by both Orpah and Naomi. We cannot determine what happens to us in life but we can choose how we react to the things that happen. Orpah reacts to her bereavement by deciding to go back to her own people and back to her own gods (1.15). This represents one way of dealing with trauma, one strategy for coping – to retreat into a private world, to cling on to what is familiar, to lower the shutters and hide. But this also represents the danger of self-pity, focusing on one's own plight, closing oneself off from other options. It is one way we can dull our pain and deaden our fears – evading the wider world, but also barricading ourselves off from the new opportunities God longs to open before us. Orpah chooses the way of retreat. It seems to offer safety and comfort but might shut the door on new possibilities for growth.

Naomi too seems backward-looking, and returns to Bethlehem partly out of a sense of nostalgia. Is she trying to turn the clock back, blotting out the painful memories of the losses she suffered in Moab, and perhaps longing for a 'golden age' in her life when she was among her own sort of people? This represents another way of coping, but it is a kind of regression, and blocks the way forward; indeed it can stunt any personal growth. When she arrives back at Bethlehem, she says to the women of the town: 'Do not call me Naomi ['Pleasant'], call me Mara ['Bitter'], for the Almighty has dealt very bitterly with me. I went away full, and the LORD has brought me back empty. Why call me Naomi, when the LORD has afflicted me and the Almighty has brought calamity upon me?' (1.20, 21). Naomi greets her bereavement with resentment; she is giving in to self-pity which can poison her relationship both with God and with others. Will jealousy surface next, as she sees the townswomen of Bethlehem standing with their husbands and grandchildren?

A pilgrimage of faith

Ruth's courageous journey from Moab to Bethlehem across the Jordan represents God's invitation to us to be pilgrims in this life. God calls us out of ourselves to adventure with him. Ruth parts from security and friends to move forwards with the God she has resolved to discover. Two characteristics shine out most clearly in Ruth's personality, that can give us clues to guide our own response to change: vulnerability and determination. First, Ruth steps out on a path of vulnerability. She is prepared for risk-taking. Perhaps she recognizes that the protective defence mechanisms adopted by the other women can in fact turn out to be barriers to God and to the future. So she will take the plunge. She has no idea what will greet her in Bethlehem, and she has left all the usual props and supports behind her, except her companion Naomi. But she moves forward in faith. She does not yet know very much about the God of Israel, but she is prepared to trust him.

Secondly, she emerges as a very determined person. It was not easy for Ruth to take this path. It was an intense struggle. She was pulled between Orpah moving back and Naomi moving out. The temptation to stay must have been enormous, and Naomi tries extremely hard to dissuade her from going with her (1.10–13). She tells Ruth plainly that she has no prospects, no hopes in coming with her. She throws at Ruth every reason to stay put. But the narrator goes on: 'And when Naomi saw that she was determined to go with her, she said no more' (1.18). Ruth was determined. She had to be so, for the pull to retreat into her private world was strong. Naomi's arguments were logical and convinced Orpah. Ruth's own family ties could not be severed easily. But Ruth realized that God sometimes asks us to let go of attachments which might hinder our growth. We need to open our eyes to what engenders and to what impedes our personal growth and be decisive. Ruth sets her sights on the distant horizon which beckons her. She anticipates the teaching of Jesus: 'No one who puts his hand to the plow and looks back is fit for the kingdom of God' (Luke 9.62).

On arrival at Bethlehem Ruth has to struggle with the experience of feeling alienated and marginalized. She immediately faces poverty and hunger. But she does not mope around in self-pity. She gets up and takes the initiative. It is harvest-time in Bethlehem, and the poor are permitted to pick up remnants of the barley left after the harvesters have passed by. Her eyes are turned towards opportunity. This recalls the words said by Jesus to the disciples when they were focusing on their own selfish need: 'I tell you, lift up your eyes, and see how the fields are already white for harvest' (John 4.35). It is this decisive lifting up of the eyes, this refusal to be downcast or self-occupied, this resolve to be awake and alert to the possibilities, that opens the way to a new future for Ruth. She is not passive but ready to do something constructive about her predicament, and prepared to work long hours, without a break, from dawn to dusk (2.7). 'So she set forth, and went and gleaned in the field after the reapers; and she happened to come to the part of the field belonging to Boaz' (2.3). 'She happened' – coincidence, chance, or is God's providence directing her steps, as she encounters Boaz? He turns out to be a kinsman, a member of her late husband's clan, a noble and generous man who greets her warmly, for he is waiting for her: '"All that you have done for your mother-in-law since the death of your husband has been fully told me, and how you left your father and mother and your native land and came to a people that you did not know before. The LORD recompense you for what you have done, and a full reward be given you by the LORD, the God of Israel, under whose wings you have taken refuge!"' (2.11, 12). Does Boaz realize that he will be used by God to fulfil the blessing he imparts to Ruth? Boaz uses the popular image of God protecting the vulnerable as an eagle shelters its young under its broad wings. But this same picture of God is also in the Israelite tradition a dynamic and powerful image of God leading his people to a new future. God says to Moses on Sinai, speaking of the experience of the Exodus: 'You have seen ... how I bore you on eagles' wings and brought you to myself' (Exodus 19.4). Ruth will find herself not only receiving protection under God's eagle wings, but also being lifted up and away to a new destiny.

At Naomi's suggestion, Ruth is to approach Boaz after his day's work, at nightfall, and to lie down at his feet as he sleeps – a tender expression of her availability to him as a partner in marriage (3.1–7). Again she takes the initiative and again she makes herself vulnerable, but Boaz does not take advantage of her. Waking up to discover her beside him, he responds with integrity and respect, covering her with his blanket until day dawns (3.8–13). He blesses her and hails her as 'a woman of worth' (3.11). Boaz must respect the local tradition which says that the next of kin has first claim to Ruth and to any inheritance that she might receive. He will not move ahead presumptuously, but holds back until the matter is properly resolved (4.1–6). In God's providence the next of kin does not wish to pursue his rightful claim, and Ruth becomes available to Boaz. As they are married, the town elders pray (4.11) that Ruth will be like Rachel and Leah 'who together built up the house of Israel' – the two wives of Jacob who shared in his struggles and crossed the Jabbok ford before him (Genesis 32.22). So Ruth becomes linked with past strugglers with God. Amazingly, her life is also to be linked with God's future plans too.

For God's providence is not finished with her yet: 'The LORD gave her conception, and she bore a son' (4.13). This gift of a son, Obed, reveals God's unfolding purposes at work, God's opening up the way to the future. Does Ruth live to hold in her arms her great-grandson? His name is David, destined to become king in Israel (4.22). The name of Ruth, the woman who ventures forth from the obscurity of Moab, will be found worthy to be included in the opening verses of Matthew's Gospel as the genealogy of Jesus himself is traced back to David and Abraham. Ruth has played a small but significant part in God's plan of salvation. She is a link in the chain that unites Jesus to the founding father of Israel. God is at work, weaving her small story into the fabric of a bigger picture which brings hope to the whole world. She has allowed herself to become caught up in the divine purposes, though at the time she did not fully glimpse this. Who can tell what might happen if we, like Ruth, embrace the changes that come our way with courage and utter openness to God?

Where can we find pointers that will help us shape a spirituality in the face of change? How can we, like Ruth, develop an outlook that is open to God's future? How can we learn to respond to change in such a way that we place ourselves within the stream of God's grace and power? We will begin with a remarkable text written in the eighteenth century, and conclude with a look at New Testament teaching on God's call to change. The classic text that can encourage us in the search for a spirituality in the face of change is *Self-Abandonment to Divine Providence* by Jean-Pierre de Caussade (1675–1751). He wrote his book to counter the heresy of Quietism, which had become popular in Europe through the works of Archbishop Fénelon and Madame Guyon. They taught that the surest way to union with God was to foster and maintain a state of utter passivity before God, to allow God to sovereignly speak and guide the soul in contemplative silence. But at its extreme, Quietism demanded a complete withdrawal from the world, the annihilation of the human will, and a cessation of all human effort, in the search to become totally available to God. De Caussade saw some truth in this approach, but also recognized the dangers. He taught that a better way is to strive for a synergy, an active co-operation with God's will, according to Paul's ideas in Romans: 'We know that in everything God works for good with those who love him, who are called according to his purpose' (8.28). De Caussade believed that God is supremely active in the world, guiding all things according to his divine plans. Our part is to be awake and responsive to God's actions, to allow him to move and direct our life in the midst of change. We are to train ourselves to recognize God's hand of providence in the 'chances and changes of this mortal life'.

The sacrament of the present moment

De Caussade gave us the striking phrase 'the sacrament of the present moment'. He teaches us that we should not live in the past nor become anxious about the future, but rather be totally available to God this day and this very moment. As Paul says, 'Behold, now is the acceptable time; behold, now is the day of salvation' (2 Corinthians 6.2). The Psalmist pleads with us: 'O that today you would hearken to his voice!' (95.7). Today, right now, God waits to meet us. How can we live with a spirit of expectancy? De Caussade urges us to live in an attitude of continual surrender to God, yielding ourselves totally to him without qualification or preconditions, so we can become channels through which he can work: 'Loving, we wish to be the instrument of his action so that his love can operate in and through us.'[1] We are to live by humble trust in God, confident that he is working his purposes out. We are not to seek our own fulfilment but God's kingdom: 'Follow your path without a map, not knowing the way, and all will be revealed to you. Seek only God's kingdom and his justice through love and obedience, and all will be granted to you.'[2] Abandoned into God's hands, we are to 'go with the flow' as he opens and closes doors before us.

How does God guide us in our decision-making and in evaluating the changes that come our way? De Caussade suggests that the secret is becoming so malleable to God's touches, with our talents and resources at God's disposal and ready for any possibility, that we can notice God speaking to us in what he calls our 'impulses': 'This is why they must always remain simple, pliant and responsive to the slightest prompting from these almost imperceptible impulses. God, who possesses them, may make use of them in any way for his glory.'[3] In another place he states: 'Intuition and inspiration are then intimations of God's will.'[4]

He encourages us to have 'a humble and willing disposition and a readiness to follow the movement of grace'.[5] But how can we be sure that we are interpreting these divine 'nudges' aright, and are not deluded? De Caussade says that while the truly surrendered soul will recognize the divine initiatives, it is wise to check these out with a soul friend or spiritual director experienced in the gift of discernment.

In this life, he says, we may not always be able consciously to recognize God's hand at work. He likens our life to a great tapestry. Here below, we may only see the reverse side of this work. As we do our tasks and fulfil our duties, facing up to our challenges, it might seem an untidy business with no clear pattern discernible:

The accomplishment of that duty is at each moment one imperceptible stitch added to the tapestry. And yet it is with these stitches that God performs wonders of which one occasionally has a presentiment at the time, but which will not be fully known until the great day of judgement.[6]

Only in hindsight may we see the pattern emerging from the tangled threads; only in heaven can we understand our life as the right side of a beautifully formed tapestry, a work of art. When we are in the thick of things, we may well be unable to recognize God's design unfolding, so it is imperative to keep on faithfully doing what is required of us in each present moment.

De Caussade reminds us that God is everywhere present and actively at work in the world fulfilling his plans but respecting human freedom and human resistance to his nudging. We are to cultivate an attitude which is alert to God's presence in the little things of life. His teaching is summed up in the striking words: 'Each moment is a revelation of God.' We do not have to hark back to the past to find God, nor wait until tomorrow. Right now God is in our midst; our task is to be vigilant and attentive to him.

But what if suffering and upheavals come our way – can these be welcomed as God's will for us? Should we not try to fight against them? De Caussade warns that we must not set bounds or limits to God's plans. He is a 'God of surprises'. He works in unpredictable and unlikely ways and we should be ready for anything: 'The terrifying objects put in our way are nothing. They are only summoned to embellish our lives with glorious adventures.'[7] Even hardships can be in God's hands pathways to growth: 'With God, the more we seem to lose, the more we gain. The more he takes from us materially, the more he gives spiritually.'[8] We should not resent difficult circumstances, but rather listen to what God is saying to us through them. We need to train ourselves to 'take advantage of every opportunity'.[9]

How then is it possible to cultivate an attitude of such openness to God? How is it possible to acquire what de Caussade calls 'the most subtle wisdom possible regarding the ways of God in this life'? He says it is achieved by living in communion with God, and allowing Jesus Christ to dwell at the very centre of our being. The Christ who longs to live within us is 'noble, loving, free, serene, and fearless'. De Caussade has a vision of the Christ-life growing within each person who has the courage to surrender to him. This is the secret of recognizing 'the sacrament of the present moment'.

When we turn to the New Testament we discover that this is precisely the invitation: to change and become more like Jesus Christ. Jesus begins his preaching with an urgent summons to change: 'The time is fulfilled, and the kingdom of God is at hand; repent, and believe in the gospel' (Mark 1.15). Today, Christ insists, the kingdom of God is within your grasp. The kingdom of God is a new way of living, in which God is truly King and sovereign, bringing order into our chaos. But to be able to embrace this possibility we have to change – the word for 'repent' meaning 'turn right round'. We have to turn from defensive self-protective strategies which pull the hatch down in times of crisis. We must instead courageously expose ourselves to God's grace and power.

Jesus is emphatic. 'He called a little child and had him stand among them. And he said: "I tell you the truth, unless you change and become like little children, you will never enter the kingdom of heaven"' (Matthew 18.3, NIV). The challenge is to change fundamentally and become like the child, ready to trust, ready to receive (Mark 10.15). This is a call to give up our natural desire to manipulate and control our own lives. It is a call to open ourselves to allow God to direct and shape our destiny. It involves a painful letting-go of our tendency to self-sufficiency.

The central struggle of the New Testament is exactly this conflict between our 'natural' human inclinations to self-centredness and our divinely-charged spiritual nature. We will explore this more fully in Chapter 9. We are pulled in different directions: as Paul puts it, 'to live according to the flesh' with a propensity to stubborn independence from God, or 'to live according to the Spirit', in tune with God's desires and will. There is a basic hostility between these two ways of living (Romans 8.7), an essential opposition.

The way forward out of the impasse is the path of transformation. Paul pleads with us: 'Do not be conformed to this world but be transformed by the renewal of your mind, that you may prove what is the will of God, what is good and acceptable and perfect' (Romans 12.2). This is the heart of the Christian message: we are invited to fundamental change within, to allow Christ's way of responding to the world to grow within us: 'Now the Lord is the Spirit, and where the Spirit of the Lord is, there is freedom. And we all, with unveiled face, beholding the glory of the Lord, are being changed into his likeness from one degree of glory to another; for this comes from the Lord who is the Spirit' (2 Corinthians 3.17, 18). As we give way more and more to the Holy Spirit, we are gradually liberated and set free from strategies which are self-destructive and impede our growth – the sort of reactions displayed by Naomi and Orpah of old. The Holy Spirit working with us delivers us from negative responses to circumstances – like strife, jealousy, envy and selfishness (Galatians 5.20, 21) – and enables us to react with the fruit of the Spirit – including patience, gentleness and self-control (Galatians 5.22, 23) which we saw emerging in the figure of Ruth. In short, Christians become more like Jesus Christ who is the model of a life lived in joyful surrender to God, and who taught us to pray, 'Your kingdom come, Your will be done.'

And this inner change, worked in us by the Spirit and modelled on Christ, empowers us to respond positively to the outer changes in the circumstances of our lives, with courage and openness. Ruth's life gives us a glimpse of the possibilities. Her experience points forward to the central invitation of the gospel: to change, to let go of the past, and to expose ourselves to the grace of the Holy Spirit and the power of Jesus Christ. It involves a struggle against our own stubbornness and inclination to be defensive, but it is also the pathway to growth and joy.

Questions for Discussion or Reflection

1. Can you recognize any defensive, self-protective strategies operating in your own life? See if you can identify alternative ways of responding to the situations you face.
2. How do you respond to the two characteristics of vulnerability and determination in Ruth? Is there a paradox here?
3. What do you think de Caussade means by 'intuition and inspiration are then intimations of God's will'? What is your experience of these?

Prayer Exercise

Either

Make a review of the last twenty-four hours in the way recommended by St Ignatius of Loyola. Ask God to help you recognize the signs of his presence during the day, and what he has been asking of you in each situation. Note down your reactions to the things that happened, your feelings at the time and what de Caussade calls 'impulses', 'intuition' and 'inspiration'. Do you feel that you were drawn in any particular direction by God in these ways? Is there any aspect of your day that stands out, where God was inviting you to change in some way? Express sorrow for any opportunities missed, or for times you defensively closed yourself off from God's nudgings. Give thanks for God's many gifts to you this day. Resolve to be alert to God tomorrow.

Or

Draw a time-line – a horizontal line marked off into decades of your life. Write in major events or changes in your life thus far. Notice God's hand of providence and guidance in what you have written – doors opening or closing, endings and new beginnings. Give thanks for the ways he has brought you through difficult times. Entrust yourself afresh to God by using Psalm 25.

Notes

1. Muggeridge, K. (tr.), *The Sacrament of the Present Moment: Jean-Pierre de Caussade*. Fount, London, 1996, p. 46.
2. Muggeridge, p. 75.
3. Muggeridge, p. 32.
4. Muggeridge, p. 77.
5. Muggeridge, p. 79.
6. Muggeridge, p. 72.
7. Muggeridge, p. 40.
8. Muggeridge, p. 54.
9. Muggeridge, p. 93.

Chapter 3

Struggling with stress

Recent research has discovered that sixty per cent of working adults have suffered from some form of stress in the last three years. Significantly, over forty per cent of those who experienced stress at work reported that this had worsened in the last year. Poor management, the relentless drive for efficiency in a competitive market-place, the setting of targets, the move towards performance-related pay, the reality that all are expendable in business, working longer hours – these have all contributed to the intensifying of pressure in the workplace. Add to this the strains created by bereavement, divorce or marital problems, illness, pregnancy, financial worry – and a cumulative burden of stress builds up in many lives today.

What then is stress? It is some form of external pressure which, if allowed to push us beyond our limits of coping, can result in overload or serious illness. It can affect every aspect of life – our behaviour, our way of reacting to others; our physical well-being, causing migraine, ulcers or heart disease; our spiritual life, making it difficult to pray and quenching our spiritual growth.

In this chapter we ask, How can we allow our encounters with the stresses of life to bring us closer to God? How can we find God in the midst of this struggle? How can stresses reveal to us what is most important in life? Can we discover ways of preventing stresses?

First of all, we turn to the towering figure of Elijah
help. He is indeed one of the greatest heroes of the Ol
Testament, but his influence is not limited to his own
time. In fact, he becomes an icon or archetype. Writing
some four hundred years after Elijah's time, the prophet
Malachi, in the last verse of the Old Testament, writes:
'Behold, I will send you Elijah the prophet before the
great and terrible day of the LORD comes. And he will
turn the hearts of the fathers to their children' (Malachi
4.5, 6). Elijah comes to represent the precursor of the
messiah. In Jewish tradition a place is set for Elijah at
every Passover meal, in expectation of his return to
usher in the age of the Kingdom. In the New Testament,
Elijah is remembered as 'strong and mighty' (Luke 1.17,
GNB), and is hailed as the greatest of all the prophets.
Jesus remembers his courageous and powerful ministry
(Luke 4.25), and Elijah appears beside Moses in the
vision of the transfiguration (Matthew 17.3). Jesus
recognizes his ministry fulfilled in the person of John the
Baptist (Matthew 17.10–13). Paul recalls his prayer in
the face of overwhelming odds (Romans 11.2–4), while
James holds him up as an example of an intercessor
whose prayer has 'great power in its effect' (James
5.16b). Yet in the narration of the first book of the
Kings, this man experiences intense struggles in his
relationship with God as a result of stress, some of it of
his own making. We can recognize in Elijah's life clues to
the wise handling of stress – and learn from his mistakes.
From him we can see what impact stress can have on our
spirituality.

He lived in one of the darkest periods of Israel's
history. The reigning king Ahab was evil (see 1 Kings
16.30) and easily manipulated by his wife Jezebel. The
daughter of a priest of a Phoenician fertility cult, she was
a cruel and domineering woman intent on promoting the
religion of her 'Baal' deities throughout the kingdom of

Israel. Elijah steps onto the scene from obscure origins. What, precisely, was the task given him by God? He is to uphold standards of righteousness in the monarchy, and confront Ahab when he strays. But Elijah seems to go beyond what is asked of him, setting himself impossible goals and so exacerbating his stressful situation.

Generating stressful situations

The warning signs are already there in the opening verses of the Elijah cycle of stories. In 1 Kings 17, he comes to speak God's word of judgement to Ahab, and immediately places himself in the firing line. God says to him: 'Depart from here and turn eastward, and hide yourself' (17.2). Jezebel will surely want an end to this troublesome prophet and God directs Elijah to a place of refuge. He finds water in the brook Cherith, on the far side of the Jordan, and is fed by ravens (17.4–7). Next, he finds a roof and food in the home of a widow of Zarephath (17.8–16). Three years after the drought began, God asks him to return to Ahab and announce rain (18.1). Elijah meets the righteous Obadiah who warns him that Ahab has hunted everywhere for him and reports that Jezebel has begun a crusade to annihilate the prophets of the God of Israel. Obadiah however informs Elijah that he has been able to hide one hundred prophets in secret caves for their protection and they are safe and well. When Elijah meets Ahab, he is hailed as 'you troubler of Israel' (18.17), but Elijah responds that it is Ahab's idolatry which has brought trouble on the nation. Elijah is seized by an ambitious plan to show up the deficiency of Jezebel's gods. Acting on his own initiative, and going way beyond the task set for him by God, he imperiously challenges Ahab to a showdown, a face-to-face contest with the prophets of Baal. Ahab is to gather the people of Israel on Mount Carmel to witness this and make their choice.

Elijah is creating for himself two problems that will heap upon him an unnecessary burden of stress. First, he seeks a confrontation, not required by God. He has set himself an impossible goal – to stamp out all Baal worship at one stroke. Though he has noble objectives, he is allowing zeal and ambition to get the better of him. In today's parlance, he becomes an idealistic, self-motivated achiever, who permits himself to be controlled by fantastically high expectations. Second, Elijah chooses to act entirely alone, in isolation, without anyone to help him. Even though Obadiah has told him that one hundred prophets are potentially available for ministry, Elijah takes on himself the task of confronting the four hundred and fifty prophets of Baal who assemble on Carmel. What stubborn streak in Elijah's personality makes him choose this solitary path? Is he intent on being a 'martyr figure' to gain for himself more admiration and respect? Is he tempted by ambition – so set on carving for himself a career as God's foremost prophet that he refuses to countenance the possibility of working with sympathetic partners? Or does he simply prefer the one-man-show to teamwork?

Whatever his motives, he stands alone before the myriad ranks of Baal's prophets assembled on Mount Carmel. He asks them to set before their deity a sacrifice of a bull placed on wooden stakes, and challenges them to call down Baal to set it alight. He sarcastically mocks his opponents (18.27) as they rant and rave for hours around their altar calling on Baal, meeting with no answer. Then he ups the stakes as he repeatedly drenches his altar to the God of Israel with water to make the task of lighting the sacrifice even more difficult. He is certainly creating stress for himself in this action, as the water soaks the sacrifice, but he calls out in confidence to God, asking him to prove himself by sending fire from heaven. When God's fire falls, the people hail the true God of Israel, and Elijah leads the false prophets away to their doom.

Signs of burn-out

Signs that mental and physical exhaustion are already catching up with him emerge as Elijah climbs the summit of Carmel to get away from the crowd. The narrator tells us that he sits down with his head in his hands. But this momentous day is not over yet. Seven times he sends his servant to look for signs of rain in the sky. Then he tells Ahab to return immediately to his base to avoid bad weather, and Elijah insists on running ahead of Ahab's chariot – over a distance of some thirty miles! On arrival, Elijah is met by a messenger from Jezebel telling him she intends to murder him within twenty-four hours.

Greeted by these words, surely Elijah's heart begins to beat fast, pumping adrenaline again through his veins. He is now faced with a choice – 'fight or flight'. Will he use his energy to struggle it out with his adversary, or will he run? He decides to flee for his life – going a considerable distance, over a hundred miles to Beersheba in the south of the country (19.1–3). There he ventures out into the Negev desert, alone. This may represent the response of escapism which is always a strong temptation for those facing excessive stress. It certainly represents a wilderness experience for Elijah, the desert symbolizing his inner state. As the winds blow across the empty plains, so a desolation sweeps over Elijah's soul. How has he descended into this state so quickly? In fact, all the warning signs were there but went unnoticed: unremitting pressure from Jezebel, a failure to delegate or work with others, impossible targets. Now Elijah is suicidal. Collapsing under a tree, he cries out to God: 'It is enough; now, O LORD, take away my life' (19.4). In these words he confesses that life now seems pointless, and he cannot see any future for himself.

Elijah displays the classic indicators of 'burn-out', a form of breakdown. He is exhausted physically, and has been pushing his body far too far. He is drained spiritually, having burnt up all his inner resources in the contest on Carmel. He is depressed and succumbs to self-pity, turned in on himself. There is disillusionment and despair, as he realizes that his victory on Carmel has not meant an end to Jezebel's plans to spread her idolatry throughout the country. It dawns on Elijah that his own goal for its instant extermination was unrealistic. He is overwhelmed by a sense of failure and powerlessness. There is a loss of self-confidence and self-esteem as he doubts his ability to continue his ministry. There is a crisis of vocation, as Elijah realizes that the task set him, the job he accepted from God, does not bring him fulfilment but frustration – there is more than a trace of anger in his words to God. And there is isolation – Elijah even separates himself from the servant who had been accompanying him (19.3). All these feelings are timeless realities, experienced in every generation. Today we can encounter them all if we take a similar path to Elijah and make the same mistakes. At least Elijah has come to a point where he can talk with God, turning his heartaches into urgent prayer. His cry to God is honest and does not attempt to hide what he is feeling. The lines of communication are open – and this opens the way to a new future.

God's response

How does God respond to his plight? God's response will give us clues for handling our own struggle with stress. There is a sense, in the account, of a clear set of priorities, an order and progression in God's plan of action for Elijah. First, God answers Elijah's physical needs of exhaustion. He gives him the gift of sleep (19.5). Then, through the agency of the angel, he gives him a hot meal and refreshing drink. Then more sleep is given. This is the first priority – to take efforts to restore the body.

Next, God invites Elijah to begin a journey (19.7). This is no ordinary journey, but a pilgrimage, for the destination is to be Mount Sinai (Horeb), 'the mount of God', the place where God revealed himself to Moses and gave him the Law. In calling Elijah to Sinai, God is drawing him back to the wellsprings and fountain of his faith. It is time for Elijah to go back to basics, to return to the foundations and the essentials of faith. So, in the strength of food given him by God, Elijah treks further south to the very place where God first gathered together the people of Israel.

When Elijah arrives at Sinai, he retreats to a cave and, hiding in a dark corner, he waits there. God asks him, 'What are you doing here, Elijah?' In these words, God is enquiring into his expectations. Is he really ready to meet God? Is he open to a renewal of his faith? Is he still self-occupied, or will he be prepared to open himself to God? We can only receive from God when we are in a place of receptivity. We need to unburden ourselves totally of the negative thinking which has been clogging us up, so we can receive the re-energizing breath of God. Twice God gives Elijah an opportunity to empty himself of his doubts and fears – to get it decisively out of his system. Elijah pours forth his inner pain like a torrent before God. What he says reveals a very stressed way of looking at things, indeed a distorted and deluded train of thought, almost paranoid in character: 'I, even I only, am left.' He has forgotten again the one hundred prophets that Obadiah plainly told him about (18.13). But this *is* prayer – honest, plain-talking prayer. In this kind of prayer, we can expose our hidden fears to God, lower our barriers before him, and truthfully share our inner turmoil. If we first do this, then we can, like Elijah, begin to receive from God the graces he wants to give.

God responds in three ways. First, he gives him a vision of himself; second, a practical plan of action, a set of priorities to guide his future; third, he corrects his false thinking.

What is the meaning of the theophany Elijah is given? 'And behold, the LORD passed by, and a great and strong wind rent the mountains, and broke in pieces the rocks before the LORD, but the LORD was not in the wind; and after the wind an earthquake, but the LORD was not in the earthquake; and after the earthquake a fire, but the LORD was not in the fire; and after the fire a still small voice' (19.11, 12). Its clearest meaning, in the context of Elijah's life, is that God is not primarily interested in proving himself in great displays of power, in impressive demonstrations – as Elijah asked him to do on Carmel. The fire, the earthquake, the wind all speak of stressful ways of working, noisy and disturbing – and God is not to be found in them. Rather he is to be discovered in the still small voice, in the silence. Elijah needs to change, indeed revolutionize his way of thinking. He must make time and space in his life so he will be able to listen and attend to God's voice speaking in the mind, the spirit, the conscience. This voice gets crowded out, drowned by incessant noise and activity. Elijah must learn the secret of stillness – to build into his ministry opportunities to be utterly silent before God, times when God is given a chance to minister to him, times when he can receive from God inner healing and a renewal of his spiritual resources. This is a vital safeguard against future burn-out.

But God gives him another safeguard against the

threat of stress. 'And when Elijah heard it, he wrapped his face in his mantle, and went out and stood at the entrance of the cave' (19.13). Elijah is now leaving his place of hiding, coming out into the open, ready to see horizons again, ready to face the future. Now God gives Elijah a very specific action plan, a clear set of priorities. He cannot take on everything at once; he must see what is important and what is not. The 'tyranny of the present moment' must pass; never again must Elijah allow himself to be overwhelmed by the enormity of his task. He must be realistic, he must plan, he must pace himself. God gives him three definite steps to take which will in fact transform the political landscape, anointing new kings for Syria and Israel. He does not need to worry right now about precisely how Ahab and Jezebel will be removed – that is in God's hands. He must be obedient to these imperatives, and everything else can wait. God's response to Elijah reminds us that goal-setting can be a valuable strategy for living without stress. Goals need to be realistic, achievable, measurable, manageable. They provide a clear focus and cut out unnecessary distractions which can sap our strength.

Moreover, God's plan includes a provision which will immediately lift the stress from Elijah: he is to anoint Elisha as his colleague and successor. He must never again work alone. Elisha will be to him a companion and a partner. Indeed, Elisha will minister to him (19.21). We may note that Elisha is not going to repeat Elijah's disastrous mistake of creating isolation. Elisha will have regular contact with the prophetic schools or guilds – the 'companies of the prophets' (see 2 Kings 2:3–7, 15–18; 4.38–44; 6.1–7). Back-up and support structures will be in place.

But God is not finished with Elijah yet. Finally, God seeks to correct his false thought-patterns. God invites him to take another look at reality, to regain the perspective he has lost. God assures Elijah that he is not alone, that there are as many as seven thousand people in Israel who have not bowed the knee to Baal (19.18). Elijah must discipline himself to apprise himself of all the relevant facts of the situation, and never again close himself off from the bigger picture. In making reference to the 7000, God is calling Elijah away from paranoia and self-pity, and to set himself in proper context.

And so Elijah comes through the struggle, with help from God and a colleague. You can read about Elijah's subsequent career in 1 Kings 21—2 Kings 2. Is there a difference in him? Has he learned his lessons? He will again face potentially stressful situations, confronting Ahab over his ruthless exploitation of Naboth, and exposing his complicity in murder. But he keeps his composure and finds a ready, penitent response in his old adversary (21.27–9). Elijah must also challenge Ahab's son about his error in consulting the foreign deities (2 Kings 1). When he sends fifty soldiers to arrest him, they find Elijah 'sitting on the top of a hill' (2 Kings 1.9). Has Elijah discovered at last a strategy for coping, a way of staying calm in the centre of the storm? Has he finally applied the lesson of making time and space for solitude, for prayer, for God in the midst of a hectic lifestyle?

Seeking a spirituality in the face of stress

To what sources can we turn in the quest for a spirituality in the face of stress? To the very mount where Elijah experienced his greatest conflict, there came Christians seeking to form a community which looked to the figure of Elijah for inspiration. First of all, a church was built on Mount Carmel about AD 500, and a monastery of Greek monks was formed. Later, Latin Christians came to Carmel in the twelfth century, seeking to pattern themselves on the positive sides of Elijah's example. They were struck by his zeal and dedication. They admired his awareness of God's presence: 'As the LORD of hosts lives, before whom I stand' (1 Kings 18.15). They interpreted Elijah's 'double spirit' asked for by Elisha (2 Kings 2.9) as representing the union of the active and contemplative life, the 'mixed life'. When in 1210 St Albert wrote for these brothers a Rule[1] to guide their developing lifestyle, he endeavoured to strike a fine balance between action and stillness. Though he was writing for the monks of Mount Carmel, his guidelines can give us too valuable clues for ordering our life aright. Albert's aim was to provide for the brothers of Carmel an integrated life, a life in which all time could be sanctified, 'pondering the Lord's law day and night'. Albert writes that 'common sense is the guide of the virtues' and he proposes a carefully disciplined lifestyle that maintains a healthy equilibrium between four pairs of opposite commitments.

First, Albert insists on a balance between solitude and community, between being alone and interacting with others. He requires: 'each of you is to have a separate cell', a space for living and praying which each monk could call his own. The Desert Fathers had taught 'Go, sit in your cell, and your cell will teach you everything.'[2] The cell becomes a symbol of the need to safeguard a space in our lives where we can be by ourselves, uninterrupted, and available to God in expectant, waiting, prayer.

Albert recognized the need to safeguard and protect from intrusion a place of privacy. There are times, he taught, that we must be entirely alone with God, as Elijah discovered, in order to listen attentively and without distraction to God. But there are also times when the community must come together, and he directs that the oratory or chapel must be 'built as conveniently as possible among the cells'. It represents the call to shared worship, the community at prayer. So too must the brothers eat in a common refectory, where they listen together to Scripture, and labour side by side at the communal tasks. The togetherness and aloneness must be held within a creative tension, the one sustaining the other.

Second, Albert proposes for the brothers on Mount Carmel a balance between work and prayer, activity and rest. He insists on the necessity of work for each of the brothers: 'You must give yourselves to work of some kind, so that the devil may always find you busy; no idleness on your part must give him the chance to pierce the defences of your souls.' Albert says of the daily round of labour that 'this is the way of holiness and goodness; see that you follow it'. But the day is to begin at the altar and be punctuated by periods of prayer. The *Rule* requires daily attendance at the Eucharist, and Carmelites see in the experience of Elijah nourished by bread from God on his pilgrimage to Sinai a sign of Communion sustaining us in daily life. In addition, there are seven times for common prayer each day – the 'canonical hours' of the Daily Office, times for recollection using psalms of praise and petition. The whole day is to be marked by an alternating cycle of work and prayer. This rhythm will prevent the build up of stress.

Third, Albert proposes for the brothers on Carmel a strict balance between silence and talking. Silence must be observed from Evening Prayer until morning. 'At other times,' he counsels, 'although you need not keep silence so strictly, be careful not to indulge in a great deal of talk, for as Scripture has it – and experience teaches us no less – sin will not be wanting where there is much talk, and he who is careless in speech will come to harm.' Once again it is a question of proper perspective and Albert gives as his maxim: 'make a balance, then, each of you'. However, Albert is careful to make provision for the sharing of problems as they arise. The greatest day of worship should be a day too of honest reflection and exchange: 'On Sundays, or other days if necessary, you should discuss matters of discipline and your spiritual welfare; and on this occasion the indiscretions and failings of the brothers, if any be found at fault, should be lovingly corrected.' There is great wisdom in this direction to deal with problems as soon as they arise, not to procrastinate – avoiding the mistakes of Elijah.

Fourth, Albert's *Rule* recommends a balance between sharing of resources and having what is needful: 'None of the brothers must lay claim to anything as his own, but your property is to be held in common; and of such things as the Lord has given you each is to receive from the prior – that is from the man he appoints for the purpose – whatever befits his age and needs.' In this prescription he delivers the brothers from possessiveness and unnecessary attachments and encourages them to live in a spirit of simplicity, accepting gratefully what is needed for well-being.

Though these words were written for the first Carmelites, they point us towards a way to live without stress today. The *Rule* is not intended for slavish imitation, but is composed in a way that takes account of individual circumstances – for example, brothers are to fast during certain periods 'unless bodily sickness or feebleness, or some other good reason, demand a dispensation from the fast; for necessity overrides every law'. Albert understands human nature and makes allowances for weaknesses. His rule of thumb is: 'See that the bounds of common sense are not exceeded.' He is aware that this will be a struggle, and is emphatic: 'you must use every care to clothe yourselves in God's armour so that you may be ready to withstand the enemy's ambush.' Albert's *Rule* invites us to examine our lives and seek a sense of wholeness. Is there, for us, a balance between the needs of body, of mind, of spirit? If anything gets out of proportion – if there is work without prayer, or interaction with others without space for solitude – stress will result. It can be prevented, however, if we apply the principles Albert advocates for those first Carmelites, who tried to apply to themselves the lessons of Elijah's life.

The *Rule of St Albert* encouraged the spread of Carmelite communities throughout Europe. But, over time, things began to get out of kilter. Stresses crept in as the balance was disrupted. When Teresa of Avila entered Carmelite life in sixteenth-century Spain, she was horrified to discover how far the *Primitive* or *Original Rule* had been distorted and corrupted. There were too many material comforts and an acquisitiveness had crept into the religious houses. But most of all she was dismayed by the imbalance between prayer and ministry. The sisters were forever leaving the enclosure to engage in 'good works' and pastoral visiting, but there was little time for solitude left. Things had got out of proportion. Teresa felt called to reform the Carmelite order and to invite her brothers and sisters to return to the basic disciplines of prayer and contemplation. She wrote: 'This, my sisters, I should like us to strive to attain: we should desire and engage in prayer, not for our enjoyment, but for the sake of acquiring this strength which fits us for service.'[3] Teresa recognized that without prayer, all our labours can be empty of meaning and of power; by prayer we are energized by God and can become channels and instruments of his grace.

John of the Cross helped Teresa in her reforms, and made Elijah's mount a symbol of the goal of prayer. In his *Ascent of Mount Carmel* he teaches that the secret of moving towards union with God is detachment, releasing our controlling grasp on things, letting go of worries, and giving up possessiveness. It is a narrow and difficult path up to the summit but 'In this nakedness the spirit finds its quietude and rest, for in coveting nothing, nothing tires it by pulling it up, and nothing oppresses it by pushing it down, because it is in the centre of its humility.'[4] He taught that this does not require a monastic withdrawal from the world, but rather an attitude of having a lightness of touch towards it. He warns us about getting trapped in an unending cycle of materialism by 'inordinate appetites', by which he means an addictive or manipulative attitude to things. There is 'joy in temporal goods', he teaches, if we allow them to lead us to God and not away from him.

If Teresa and John's aim was to insist on specific times of stillness and solitude, another Carmelite teacher provides us with tools to build a spirituality in the very midst of daily work, bringing God's peace and perspective into every minute of the day. Brother Lawrence (1605–91) lived in France through the turbulent reign of Louis IV. After serving as a soldier, he became a lay Carmelite brother in Paris. He had a range of duties and responsibilities to deal with – engaging in business on behalf of the community, labouring in the workshop, and serving in the kitchen 'to which he had a natural aversion'.[5]

He discovered a way of living that suggests to us a strategy for preventing the build up of stress – what he called 'the practice of the presence of God'. It is an everyday application of Christ's words: 'Abide in me, and I in you' (John 15.4). It is at once a mystical but practical message – cultivate at all times an unbroken awareness of God within yourself, and continually refer all your actions to him.

The aim is to maintain a consciousness of God's

presence in the very depth of the being, and to respond to situations, as they arise, out of this inner centre of stillness. Activities should be started, developed and concluded in God: 'In the matter of this inner gaze, special care must be taken that it comes before, be it but momentarily, your outer actions, that at times it goes with them, and that you end them all in like manner.'[6] Every task and responsibility should be deliberately offered to God and completed in partnership with God. This echoes what Paul said about being 'co-workers with God'. He put it: 'By the grace of God I am what I am, and his grace toward me was not in vain. On the contrary, I worked harder than any of them, though it was not I, but the grace of God which is with me' (1 Corinthians 15.10).

Lawrence advises us that we should attempt no task whatever without placing it into God's hands and resolve: 'Whatever happens, I will do everything I do, for the rest of my life, out of love for God.'[7] He teaches us how to slow down in our reactions to situations: 'We must do all that we do with thoughtfulness and consideration, without impetuosity or haste, both of which show an undisciplined spirit; we must work quietly, placidly and lovingly before God, and pray to him to approve our toil.'[8] How can we so pace ourselves? 'We must, during our all labour and in all else we do, ... pause for some short moment, as often indeed as we can, to worship God in the depth of our heart, to savour him.'[9] Lawrence invites us to punctuate each hour with short conscious acts of praise or petition or, if needed, penitence – he tells us to deal with our sins or mistakes as soon as they arise, and not let them build up and up. It is a question of developing a mindfulness of God – not in a sanctimonious or pious way, but in an entirely natural way. Lawrence calls it 'a simple attentiveness and an habitual, loving turning of my eyes on him'.[10]

He admits it takes perseverance to discipline oneself to

live in this way – in fact, he calls it a 'revolution', because it is a radical re-ordering and re-orientation of the way we live, and so contrary to society's emphasis on self-sufficiency and independence. It is a fundamental dependence on God at every single moment, making 'a chapel of the heart'.[11] It enables the disarming of stress before it strikes, because the God within us is a reservoir of calm to be drawn upon if external tensions rise. One of his letters even contains advice for a soldier in the heat of battle: 'A small lifting of the heart suffices, a small remembrance of God, a movement of the heart's worship, though in haste and with sword in hand, are prayers . . . most pleasing to God, and, far from making those engaged in battle lose their courage, in the most dangerous moments they make them brave . . . It is a way most fitting and most necessary for a soldier, daily exposed to dangers in his life.'[12]

Lawrence's teaching suggests a spirituality for everyday living in a stressful world. Awareness of God within is to fuel and resource our reactions to every situation. Constant remembrance of God enables us to 'serve God in a holy liberty and do one's work faithfully without distress or anxiety, calling the soul gently and quietly back to God so soon as we find it drawn away from him'.[13] It enables faith to overcome fear and hope to swamp worry. This way, says Lawrence, 'faith becomes more alive and active in all the processes of our life'.[14]

In this chapter we have explored the timeless struggle with stress, beginning with the example of Elijah. Tracing a spiritual lineage from Elijah to the Carmelite tradition, we have identified the safeguards Albert taught, and seen how Teresa struggled to re-establish balance and wholeness. A later Carmelite brother suggests how we may practically implement this in the conduct of our lives. We end with the great Carmelite of the nineteenth century, Thérèse of Lisieux, who reminds us of the essence of prayer: 'For me, prayer is an aspiration of the heart, it is a simple glance directed to heaven, it is a cry of gratitude and love in the midst of trial as well as joy; finally, it is something great, supernatural, which expands my soul and unites me to Jesus.'[15]

Questions for Discussion or Reflection

1. What strains threaten your life right now? Identify clearly what stresses you. What lessons can you apply from Elijah's experience to your own situation?
2. Take another look at the four pairs of commitments considered by St Albert. What do they say to your lifestyle? Do you need to make any changes?
3. How can you implement the guidelines of Brother Lawrence?

Prayer Exercise

Either

Prayerfully review your life by drawing up a weekly 'time budget'. On the left of a sheet of paper list the following activities: time alone with God for prayer; corporate worship; employment; commuting; meals; sleep; exercise; quality time with family or friends; administration; domestic chores; other responsibilities; shopping; television/Internet; other times of relaxing or developing creativity; time alone with God in prayer; Bible study or spiritual reading; other reading or study. On the right side of the page, opposite each entry, jot down the hours per week devoted to each element. Reflect on the results: is there balance and are things in the right proportion? Do some things need to be cut? Do some things need to be increased or added? On the back of your sheet write down three resolutions and three corresponding points for

action. Finally surrender these to God in prayer, using part
of the hymn written by John Whittier:

> Drop Thy still dews of quietness,
> till all our strivings cease;
> take from our souls the strain and stress,
> and let our ordered lives confess
> the beauty of Thy peace.
>
> Breathe through the heats of our desire
> Thy coolness and Thy balm;
> let sense be dumb, let flesh retire;
> speak through the earthquake, wind, and fire,
> O still small voice of calm!

Or

Read Mark 1.14–38, which chronicles twenty-four
hours in the life of Jesus. What stresses and expectations
did he face? Note how many times Mark uses the word
'immediately' to convey a sense of the unremitting
pressures Jesus faced. How did he safeguard himself
against stress? Compare John's perspective in John
5.19–20. What is Jesus' secret? Conclude by saying
slowly the Lord's Prayer, noting how it holds many
elements of life in a careful balance.

Notes

1. Excerpts are from *The Rule of St Albert* translated
   by Bede Edwards ODC in Obbard, E. R., *Land of
   Carmel*. Gracewing, Leominster, 1999.
2. Ward, B. (tr.), *The Sayings of the Desert Fathers*.
   Cistercian Publications, Kalamazoo, 1984, p. 139.
3. Peers, E. A. (tr.), *St Teresa of Avila: Interior Castle*.
   Sheed & Ward, London, 1974, p. 148.
4. Kavanaugh, K. and Rodriguez, O. (trs.), *The
   Collected Works of St John of the Cross*. Institute of

Carmelite Studies, Washington DC, 1991, p. 111.

5. Blaiklock, E. M. (tr.), *Brother Lawrence: The Practice of the Presence of God*. Hodder & Stoughton, London, 1981, p. 23.
6. Blaiklock, p. 75.
7. Blaiklock, p. 86.
8. Blaiklock, pp. 68, 69.
9. Blaiklock, p. 69.
10. Blaiklock, p. 44.
11. Blaiklock, p. 41.
12. Blaiklock, pp. 48, 49.
13. Blaiklock, p. 40.
14. Blaiklock, p. 76.
15. Carey, T. (ed.), *Therese of Lisieux: A Discovery of Love: Selected Spiritual Writings*. New City Press, New York, 1992, pp. 93–4.

For Further Reading

Hartley, M., *The Good Stress Guide*. Sheldon, London, 1995.

McGreal, W., *At the Fountain of Elijah: The Carmelite Tradition*. Darton, Longman & Todd, London, 1999.

Welch, J. W., *The Carmelite Way: An Ancient Path for Today's Pilgrim*. Gracewing, Leominster.

Chapter 4

Struggling with anger

> O LORD, thou hast deceived me,
>   and I was deceived;
> thou art stronger than I,
>   and thou hast prevailed.
> I have become a laughingstock all the day;
>   every one mocks me.
>
> Jeremiah 20.7–9

These agonized lines from Jeremiah are the earliest expression in the Bible of an intensely personal diatribe against God. They reveal depths of pain and anger directed against God, and can be translated 'You have seduced me, Yahweh, and I have let myself be seduced; you have overpowered me' (JB). Never before had any writer dared to express himself so honestly and transparently. Jeremiah helps us look at a crucial area of struggle in the spiritual life – perhaps the great unmentionable – how do I handle anger against God? How can I turn it into prayer? How can we express ourselves when we feel betrayed or disappointed by God? How can we enable anger to be transformed into something positive, even creative?

Why is Jeremiah, writing in the seventh century BC, the first in the Bible to reveal so clearly his doubts and frustrations against God? Why was this not expressed before? And what holds us back? Was there, and is there, a feeling that it is improper to address God in this way, that it is irreverent, it is simply 'not done'? The attitude still prevails that declares we may only talk to God with deference – we must be restrained, controlled, and watch what we say to the Almighty. If this is the case, we are still inhibited from being our true selves before God. Jeremiah's *Confessions*, as they are called, (recorded in 11.18–23; 12.1–6; 15.10–21; 17.14–18; 18.18–23; 20.7–12, 14–18) invite us into a fresh encounter with God, in which we can lay bare to him our deepest doubts and disappointments.

Jeremiah was a reluctant prophet. He did not choose his vocation – rather he responded to the call with grave hesitations (1.1–6). It was a time of frightening insecurity for the people of Israel, with successive political and religious crises. The kingdoms of Judah and Israel were under threat of invasion and liquidation, reduced to being a buffer state between the armies of Egypt and Babylon. It was Jeremiah's task to warn his people of imminent danger, and to call them urgently back to God. For this he paid a heavy price. Rejected and derided by the people he loved, Jeremiah was accused of sedition, persecuted and imprisoned. Outcast and isolated, he had even been forbidden by God to marry (16.1–4). Jeremiah emerges as an outstanding man of great courage and tenacity, sensitive to criticism but brave in delivering a unpalatable message. For forty years and through the reigns of five kings he endured acute hardship. Why was it that when Jesus asked his disciples who they thought he really was, some answered 'People say you are Jeremiah come back to life!' (Matthew 16.14)? Was it because Jesus and Jeremiah shared the same characteristics of courage and love for their people?

On the face of it, Jeremiah had every reason to complain to God. First, there were his self-doubts and the questions thrown up by his damaged self-image. He was inwardly grieved to deliver a message of judgement to the people he cherished. He naturally recoiled against interpreting the unfolding political events as punishments from God to an apostate people. Greeted by abuse, indifference and gossip, he was frequently tempted to give up, to quit. Worn down by a sense of personal failure, he lost all confidence in himself. He described himself as 'a gentle lamb led to the slaughter' (11.19). Jeremiah has been called 'the prophet of the broken heart' and 'the most human of the prophets'.

Second, Jeremiah's complaints concerned the nature of God himself, and his image or picture of God was becoming distorted. Jeremiah felt duped, cheated and betrayed by God. Called to be God's spokesman, he felt so alone and deserted by God in the tragedies he faced. The God whom once he had hailed as 'the fountain of living waters' (2.13) had become 'a deceitful brook, like waters that fail' (15.18), like a gorge where the rains full of the promise of refreshment disappear before your eyes. He therefore has every right, it seems, to express his hurt freely and with emotion to this God who seemed so mystifying and incomprehensible.

We can identify with Jeremiah because we sometimes share with him the experience of disillusionment. God seems distant, prayers seem to go unanswered, comfort is elusive. It appears God is locked up in a faraway heaven. And like Jeremiah, we sometimes feel trapped and caught up into a situation from which there seems no escape. Perhaps we feel, like him, that the odds are stacked against us. Jeremiah's experience offers us hints for a spirituality of struggle – a way of praying through our times of anguish.

First, Jeremiah gives us, as it were, permission to rave against God! He says it is OK to complain. He is ground-breaking in this, smashing any taboos that forbade such talk. His *Confessions* were not cut out by the Biblical censors or editors, those who assembled and agreed the canon of Scripture. They were left in, to remind us that such expression of doubt against God does have a part to play in prayer.

Second, Jeremiah reminds us that it is essential to be totally honest with God. Our relationship with God should be unequivocal. There should be no wearing of masks, no pretending, no false pleasantries in our prayers. Jesus calls us to worship 'in spirit and in truth' (John 4.24). There is no point in deceiving ourselves or God if there is hurt in our hearts. It must be faced.

Third, Jeremiah reminds us that anger needs to be expressed. It is a catharsis, an emptying, of the inner pain. The alternative is to internalize it, to turn it within, to bottle it up. Anger suppressed becomes an inner acid of bitterness and resentment that can poison all our relationships. Paul advises, 'Be angry but do not sin; do not let the sun go down on your anger' (Ephesians 4.26). Jeremiah's secret is that he turns anger and frustration into prayer. His rage is not turned destructively within, but is freely released through prayer. Thus prayer becomes a way to experience freedom from inner captivities. Anger and turmoil when they are brought out into the open are also exposed to God's grace. When we have emptied ourselves of negativities, we have created a space within, as it were, where we can receive God's healing – there is room for God's Spirit to act. Jeremiah finds himself praying 'Heal me, O LORD, and I shall be healed' (17.14).

Fourth, Jeremiah tells us that it is the open heart that matters most before God. In an age when people were tempted to hide behind the cover of belonging to 'the people of God' and relationship with God was seen more in national and corporate terms than in personal terms, Jeremiah's words and witness speak of how crucial it is that we come to God one by one. He teaches us by his own painful example, that we need to expose our heart's hurts to God, and allow God to deal with our inner pain. He says: 'The heart is deceitful above all things, and desperately corrupt: who can understand it?' But he goes on immediately to express God's response: 'I the LORD search the mind and try the heart' (17.9, 10). Jeremiah recognizes that God alone fully understands the agonies of the human heart and he alone can transform it: 'I will put my law within them, and I will write it upon their hearts' (31.33).

Fifth, Jeremiah himself glimpses a way through the turmoil. Our opening passage from Chapter 20 goes on to express words of hope. After Jeremiah has thrown at God his hurt, he then is able to say: 'But the LORD is with me ... Sing to the LORD: praise the LORD! For he has delivered the life of the needy from the hand of evildoers' (20.11, 13; compare Romans 8.31–6). Jeremiah was able to recognize that times of anguish would not go on indefinitely – they would have an end. He senses the bigger picture, the wider perspective, which delivered him from the temptation and the danger of self-pity. He was able to look up to God and catch sight of possibilities of healing and restoration, for himself and for his people (Chapters 30–33). This kept him going. Still he trusted in the darkest hour; faith triumphed over despair.

Finally, Jeremiah reveals something about the heart of God himself. Even when he seems faraway, he *is* close by, perhaps in hidden ways. Jeremiah frequently expresses God's own anguish over his people:

You shall say to them this word:
'Let my eyes run down with tears night and day,
    and let them not cease,
for the virgin daughter of my people is smitten with
    a great wound,
    with a very grievous blow.' (14.17)

Cannot God himself be *in* the heartbreak? Jeremiah's writings reveal a God who can be grieved and pained by suffering and apostasy, a God who is close to the broken-hearted. God never promised Jeremiah an easy ride, but he did promise that he would always be *with* him (1.19). God's presence was not always obvious, but he was *within* the tears Jeremiah shed. And so Jeremiah finds that he cannot, in fact quit:

> If I say, 'I will not mention him,
>   or speak any more in his name,'
> there is in my heart as it were a burning fire
>   shut up in my bones,
> and I am weary with holding it in,
>   and I cannot. (20.9)

However desolate he might feel, he cannot walk out on God, or on the job he has been given to do. He will survive!

Songs of the heart

Jeremiah's candid and honest declarations before God pave the way for a new freedom and transparency in man's relationship with God. Now even the darkest emotions can be revealed, the unthinkable, the unspeakable can be uttered. This capacity for exposing the heart's hidden hurts finds greatest expression in the Psalms, the hymnbook of Israel. Side by side with psalms celebrating thanksgiving and praise, are desperate *cris de coeur* which explode with grief and a sense of spiritual confusion. Expressions of faith and shrieks of anguish co-exist cheek by jowl in this collection of songs used by Jewish and Christian communities through the centuries. That very fact reminds us of the necessary place of expressions of confusion and anger in a healthy spirituality. In fact, over one third of all the psalms include some kind of complaint against God.

There are community laments (e.g. 10, 74, 79, 106) which throw at God a corporate sense of despair, and there are individual complaints which reveal more personal dilemmas of faith. They speak of God's forgetting his people, God's seeming inaction, of the feeling of being abandoned by him. The idea of God as a rock or a refuge is called into question. Some psalms speak of prolonged stress:

How long, O LORD? Wilt thou forget me for ever?
    How long will thou hide thy face from me?
                                        (Psalm 13.1)

But a striking thing about many of these heart-rending psalms is the way in which there seems to be a movement from despair to hope, from anger and outrage at God to a renewed confidence in him. Psalm 22 begins with the cry taken up by Christ on the Cross (Mark 15.34):

My God, my God, why hast thou forsaken me?

but it does not stop here. Soon the psalmist recalls God's providence in the past:

Yet thou art he who took me from the womb;
    thou didst keep me safe upon my mother's breasts

and concludes with a testimony of God's support:

and he has not hid his face from him,
    but has heard, when he cried to him.

Similarly, Psalm 42 begins with plea and complaint:

> As a hart longs
>   for flowing streams,
> so longs my soul
>   for thee, O God.
> My soul thirsts for God,
>   for the living God.
> When shall come and behold
>   the face of God?
> My tears have been my food
>   day and night,
> while men say to me continually,
>   'Where is your God?'

But the psalm goes on:

> These things I remember,
>   as I pour out my soul:
> how I went with the throng,
>   and led them in procession to the house of God.

There is a vacillation, a pulling this way and that:

> Why are you cast down, O my soul,
>   and why are you disquieted within me?
> Hope in God; for I shall again praise him,
>   my help and my God.

The key to overcoming depression and a sense of despair in these psalms lies in remembering – remembering God's mercies in the past, remembering his 'steadfast love' which is his covenant-love, pledged and promised for ever. Self-pity focuses only on the immediate distress and stops there, but genuine complaint is more open-ended – it is prepared to widen its view, to recall past blessings, and recover a sense of God's unchanging faithfulness. Look up other examples and trace the movement from anger to hope in Psalms 6, 13, 35 and 102.

There are other psalms which wrestle with man's most agonizing questions: Why do the innocent suffer? What is the point of life? These are sometimes called the 'wisdom psalms' because they try to make sense of suffering and do not shy away from the most perplexing dilemmas (e.g. 1, 37, 49). Sometimes it is possible to trace a journey into deeper faith through these honest reflections. Psalm 73 begins with a sense of bitter envy of the prosperity and success of the wicked. They seem to thrive while the God-fearing ones suffer (verses 3–12), and the psalmist wonders what is the point of faith when all he knows is trouble (verses 2, 13–14). He casts doubt on the traditional teaching that the wicked cannot know success – they patently do! He dares to ask whether an upright life is worth the effort. Does believing in God make no difference to things? A sense of anger is simmering just below the surface of these doubts. He realizes that his painful questions go against the tide of faith, they are contrary to the values of his people (verse 15). Just when he seems overwhelmed by the sense of being cheated by God and unrewarded for his righteous living, he ventures into worship:

> But when I thought how to understand this,
>   it seemed to me a wearisome task,
>   until I went into the sanctuary of God. (73.16)

What transpires in the course of worship, what the theme of the celebration is, we do not know. But something happens to him – he reaches a breakthrough smashing the impasse in his thinking; he sees things in a new perspective, and he remembers half-forgotten truths. First, he realizes that the wicked enjoy only a fleeting, dream-like success. But more profoundly, he comes to see the life of faith in a new light. God does not promise material success, but he does promise something far more precious and beautiful:

> Nevertheless I am continually with thee;
>> thou dost hold my right hand.
> Thou dost guide me with thy counsel,
>> and afterward thou wilt receive me to glory.
> Whom have I in heaven but thee?
>> And there is nothing upon earth that I desire besides
>> thee.
> My flesh and my heart may fail,
>> but God is the strength of my heart and my portion
>> for ever. (73.23–6)

In these words the psalmist wakes up to the most important thing that there is – something that gives meaning and purpose in the midst of all circumstances – his relationship with God. Robert Davidson notes:

> But it is not merely the psalmist's conclusion which is interesting, it is why he reached this conclusion. If he had never been compelled by a clear-headed analysis of experience to question the traditional teaching which nurtured him; if he had not been driven to doubt whether faith had any value at all, he would never have broken through to a deeper faith. It was his doubts, his unanswered questions, and his honest and agonising attempt to deal with them, which proved to be spiritually productive. For this man doubt, far from being destructive of faith, was the midwife at the birth of a more compelling faith.[1]

Towards a spirituality in the face of anger

How far have we come? We have recognized that honest complaint has a place in our prayers, not in self-pity but in looking to God with a mixture of puzzlement and hope. We have discovered that the expression of anger can leave a space within us, as it were, that can be filled with memories of God's mercy, opening us to take another look at the situation.

Perhaps the greatest exponent of this type of spirituality is the Anglican poet-priest of the seventeenth century, George Herbert. He wrote that his poems were 'a picture of the many spiritual conflicts that have passed betwixt God and my soul'. His poems testify to an ongoing struggle to accept God's unconditional love. Herbert was born in 1593 to an aristocratic family. After studies at Cambridge University he became a lecturer in Rhetoric and for seven years held the prestigious post of Public Orator to the university. He seemed destined for high office, and set his hopes on a privileged career in the royal court, but God had other plans for him. Secular ambitions wrestled with a persistent and nagging sense of vocation to the priesthood, and Herbert finally gave in and was ordained deacon in 1626. But things were not to be straightforward for him. Illness and indecision delayed Herbert from entering full-time ministry and he was not ordained priest until 1630. Some of Herbert's most poignant and questioning poems were composed during these four 'wilderness' years. Herbert found himself appointed to a small and undistinguished parish church at Bemerton near Salisbury, and to a vicarage in a state of dilapidation.

For just three years he was to exercise his ministry, until his death in 1633. He embraced the life of a parish priest with extraordinary devotion and dedication, and expressed his ideals for pastoral ministry in his work *The Country Parson*. He even found it possible to provide a place in his home for three orphaned nieces, even though he was on greatly reduced means. But he faced different struggles during this period. Now he was no longer fighting against his vocation but, dogged with ill-health, found himself questioning his usefulness. Though he valued the presence of Christ in the scriptures and in the sacraments, he wrestled with a sense of spiritual confusion, the dilemma of unanswered prayer, and found himself echoing the sentiments of Jeremiah and the psalmists. In 'Affliction I' he tells the story of his spiritual journey:

> When first thou didst entice to thee my heart,
> I thought the service brave[2]

He experienced a time of happiness in God's service:

> What pleasures could I want, whose King I served,
> Where joys my fellows were?

But joys passed to sorrows as he encountered both physical and spiritual distress, and having had enough, he explodes with anger to God:

> Well, I will change the service, and go seek
> Some other master out.

He repeats this sense of desperation at God in the poem 'The Collar':

> I struck the board, and cried, No more;
> I will abroad.
> What? shall I ever sigh and pine?

After complaining that his only harvest is one of thorns, and his spiritual life is seemingly fruitless, he pauses and catches the echo of God's voice:

> But as I raved and grew more fierce and wild
> > At every word,
> Me thought I heard one calling, *Child*;
> > And I replied, *My Lord*.

Though his spiritual life might be turbulent, underpinning it all is the fundamental, unchangeable reality: he is God's child, and he is held in God's love. In 'Longing' he comes to see this clearly as the basic truth of his identity. After laying bare his soul's torments, he confesses that to him God is absent, aloof, far away and unresponsive:

> With sick and famish'd eyes,
> With doubling knees and weary bones,
> > To thee my cries
> > To thee my groans,
> To thee my sighs, my tears ascend:
> > > No end?
> ... Thou tarriest, while I die,
> And fall to nothing: thou dost reign
> > And rule on high
> > While I remain
> In bitter grief; yet am I styled
> > > Thy child.

The foundation of his spiritual life is secure in this abiding knowledge, though the building may sway and rock in the winds of his doubts. Herbert is surprised again and again at the wonder of God's Incarnation in Christ, which seems to break into his consciousness at his bleakest moments: the reality that God comes to us

to share our pain in the life and death of Jesus. In
'Redemption', he pictures himself as a tenant seeking to
submit a petition to his Lord:

> In Heaven at his manor I him sought:
> > They told me there, that he was lately gone.

So Herbert looks for God amidst the privileged places of
society which he himself had known so well: 'in cities,
theatres, gardens, parks, and courts'. But God is not to
be found here.

> At length I heard a ragged noise and mirth
> Of thieves and murderers: there I him espied,
> Who straight, *Your suit is granted* said, and died.

God waits to be discovered in the most unlikely places,
amidst social outcasts, sinners and well within the arena
of suffering. Christ tells us that he waits to meet us in
the hungry, the thirsty, the stranger, the naked, the sick
and even in the imprisoned villain (Matthew 25.35–40).
All these, he says, are 'my brethren'. In this poem,
Herbert finds his Lord not in places of security and
beauty, but upon a rough-hewn cross. God is not
remote from suffering but in the midst of it. As he puts
it in 'Affliction III':

> My heart did heave, and there came forth,
> *O God!*
> By that I knew that thou wast in the grief,
> To guide and govern it to my relief.

In his powerful composition 'The Cross' Herbert
comes to realize that the paradoxes of his life are,
indeed, cross-shaped. He reaches the limit of his own
strivings:

> And then when after much delay,
> Much wrestling, many a combat, this dear end,
> So much desired, is given, to take away
> 　　My power to serve thee: to unbend
> All my abilities, my designs confound,
> And lay my threatnings bleeding on the ground.

His angers, his frustrated plans, and the experience of being pulled in different directions all meet in the Cross. Indeed, on the Cross God has already enfolded and experienced them; he has *felt* them:

> Ah, my dear Father, ease my smart!
> These contrarieties crush me: these cross actions
> Do wear a rope about, and cut my heart:
> 　　And yet since these thy contradictions
> Are properly a Cross felt by thy Son,
> With but four words, my words, *Thy will be done.*

These insights help us to shape a spirituality of struggle in the face of anger and disillusionment. As in some of the psalms, Herbert is able to register a movement in his poems from complaint to acceptance, from rebellion to submission. In his struggles he discovers crucial things about God and man that cannot be learnt from textbooks and sermons, but only from the experience of struggle.

About man: that we are called to walk by faith, not by sight (2 Corinthians 5.7). We are called to tread a path of costly discipleship, not to luxuriate in self-absorption. Jesus calls us to take up our cross daily and follow him (Mark 8.34). We never cease to be loved by God, wanted by God as his child, even when we do not feel his presence. Facts, not feelings, should guide our Christian pilgrimage. When tempted to give up, we should return to the basics, go back to the fundamental reality that no distress can ever fully take away: I am God's child.

About God: Herbert reminds us that God is inscrutable, which means that he is annoying and baffling, as he is beyond the limits of our logic and reason. God constantly surprises us. Everything seems upside down, topsy-turvy in God's ways. He, the mighty one, is to be found precisely in the midst of suffering ones. God himself embraces suffering on the Cross and declares himself to be our brother. In prayer, we bring our puzzlement and wonder to God and find our attitudes transformed.

Questions for Discussion or Reflection

1. What angers or frustrations face you right now?
2. In what ways can 'the prayer of anger' be expressed? Consider symbolic and sacramental ways.
3. What is your experience of receiving a sense of peace or reassurance in the midst of trouble or distress?

Prayer Exercise

Either

Use your hands expressively in this prayer-time. Begin by clenching your fists tight and holding them before you. Feel the tension and let these fists represent an anger or frustration that bothers you today. Hold them before God. Secondly, slowly open your down-turned palms and let go of the tension. Let it fall away from you to God. In this gesture give to God any negative feelings or stresses, feel them drip out of your fingertips, as it were. Finally, turn your hands upwards in a gesture of surrender to God and of receiving from God. Breathe in what God wants to give you right now – perhaps a reassurance that all will be well, or a sense of his peace. Be thankful that you can empty yourself before God and receive from him.

Or

Find a symbolic way of expressing your anger: throwing stones into the sea, or more easily at home, write out on a piece of paper your current frustration with God (briefly!). Crush it up into a ball and cast it into a wastepaper bin placed in front of a cross. Let this be a way of throwing at God the frustration you have identified. Then spend some moments silently looking at the cross above the bin. See there how Christ enfolds the world's troubles and your own strife. And give thanks.

Notes

1. Davidson, R., *The Courage to Doubt: Exploring an Old Testament Theme*. SCM Press, London, 1983, p. 36.
2. The definitive collection of poems is Hutchinson, F. E. (ed.), *The Works of George Herbert*. Clarendon Press, Oxford, 1970.

For Further Reading

Sheldrake, P., *Love Took My Hand: The Spirituality of George Herbert*. Darton, Longman & Todd, London, 2000.

Chapter 5

Struggling with suffering

There is no struggle more painful in our relationship with God than that of trying to come to terms with suffering and loss. It cuts right at the heart of our faith, and any spirituality we develop must sooner or later attempt to find some meaning in the experience of pain and bereavement.

The book of Job is presented as a drama which faces up to the problem of innocent suffering. We do not know if Job actually was an historical character, but he is set before us as a representative figure, standing for people in every age who cry out 'Why? Why does God allow such suffering?' Sometimes we hear references today to 'the patience of Job' but this conjures up a false picture of him. He does not emerge as a person who accepts suffering passively, patiently, submissively. Rather he is presented as a true-to-life character who argues fiercely with God and struggles hard to make sense of his plight. What happens to him? Does he discover any answers? Can he point us in the right direction, so that we too can find a way to pray through our suffering?

At the outset, Job is described as a man who has everything. He is blessed with a family of seven daughters and three sons. He owns vast properties and possessions. In fact he is described as 'the greatest of all the people of the east' (1.3). But there is complacency in the air – at least among his children who seem to spend most of their time feasting in each others' houses, wine overflowing. Yet Job is presented as a God-fearing man, though his relationship with God is a formal one, sealed by Job's daily ritual of offering sacrifices – burnt offerings – to God for each of his children. This looks like a kind of insurance policy – to appease God for any indulgences or oversights of his children, and to stay God's hand of judgement against them. The question arises (1.9–11), does Job only respect God because all is going well for him? What if he did not have such luxury and possessions, would he still honour God?

Within a few days, Job loses everything. First his possessions are stolen by raids of thieves, his servants are murdered and then his children are killed by a seemingly-freak tornado which crushes the house they were partying in. Then Job's health is overtaken by a mysterious illness which afflicts him with sores all over his body. He is left alone with only his wife to pick up the pieces of his shattered life. At first, it seems, Job is prepared to accept his lot philosophically, but his wife cannot let this go unquestioned:

> Then his wife said to him, 'Do you still hold fast your integrity? Curse God, and die.' But he said to her, 'You speak as one of the foolish women speak. Shall we receive good at the hand of God, and shall we not receive evil?' (2.9, 10)

But his wife is right. He cannot hold on to this unqualified belief for long. The suffering is intolerable, devastating. Can God really want this for his children?

Job has bottled up his confusion and hurt; he has tried to keep a lid on it. He has persisted in niceties in his prayers to God. But then all is unleashed:

> After this Job opened his mouth and cursed the day of his birth.

And Job said:
'Let the day perish wherein I was born,
   and the night which said,
'A man-child is conceived.'
   Let that day be darkness!' (3.3)

Then Job gives vent to the biggest question of all: 'Why?'

'Why did I not die at birth,
   come forth from the womb and expire?' (3.11)

Job asks why he has become the victim of his recent
devastating circumstances. What purpose can there
possibly be in this? Job's 'Why?' is the timeless question
that surfaces in a million hearts today. Why do children
die through warfare? Why do innocent people perish
through 'natural disaster'? Why am I suffering with this
illness right now? Where's the sense in it?

Searching for meaning in suffering

Job is visited by three friends, his so-called 'comforters'.
Their dialogue is recorded in three cycles, in which each
of them speaks, and Job responds. What answers can
they offer him? Eliphaz and his colleagues emerge as
inflexible, dogmatic advice-givers. They trot out the only
answer they have discovered, the traditional explanation
which has been handed down to them. Their position is
introduced in Chapters 3 and 4, and is reiterated in
different ways throughout the book. It has almost
become a formula, an equation: 'righteous people
flourish; wicked men perish; therefore it follows that the
suffering one must have sinned'. The 'friends' conclude
that Job must have sinned, and see his plight as God's
judgement on him. Cold comfort!
But the logic of this position finds an echo even today

in popular sayings: 'All these things are sent to try us!' and 'What have I done to deserve this?' The first presupposes a God who likes to 'send' trials – not only allowing these things to happen but also originating them. The second saying implies not only a God who judges wrong-doing but one who visits punishments from heaven in retribution or correction. However crude these perspectives seem, they gained currency in Job's time and they persist today.

But they will not do, and Job knows they will not do. They imply a horrendous view of God, and do not accord with experience, for sufferings do not seem like 'the punishment that fits the crime'. Job's comforters can offer only inadequate answers, and they cannot account for the suffering of the innocent. Job is prepared to rebuff them on two counts. First, he questions the authenticity of the received wisdom of his friends. He asks them,

> 'Why do the wicked live,
>   reach old age, and grow mighty in power?' (21.7)

Job points out that it is simply not true that wickedness is punished in this life, for the evidence seems to be the opposite. The world is full of corrupt and exploiting people who seem to escape calamity and thrive. Second, Job does not believe he has done anything which merits such devastating judgement from God. He is prepared to defend his corner, and protests his innocence as his friends keep on insinuating that he has deserved his lot:

> 'Far be it from me to say that you are right;
>   till I die I will not put away my integrity from me.
> I hold fast my righteousness, and will not let it go;
>   my heart does not reproach me for any of my days.'
>   (27.5, 6)

Is Job blinded with pride, self-righteously unaware of his possible sin? No, his conscience is clear: he genuinely believes he has always acted with integrity and compassion to others:

> 'I was eyes to the blind,
>   and feet to the lame,
> I was a father to the poor.' (29.15, 16a)

In the midst of his struggle, his moods vacillate between suicidal despair and hope in God. In his darkest moments, he thinks of God as his enemy, and he can accuse God of injustice. Job can be ruthlessly honest in his relationship with God (see Chapters 27–30). Though broken by suffering and undermined by so-called friends, he does cling to his relationship with God, and can even cry out: 'I know that my Redeemer lives, and at last he will stand upon the earth' (19.25). Most significant of all, while his friends are stuck in a rut in their thinking, Job is prepared to move forwards. He can accept that some good can come out of his plight, that from the crucible of suffering can come some redemptive possibilities: 'When he has tried me, I shall come forth as gold' (23.10). Nevertheless, Job is longing for a deeper understanding, for an encounter with his elusive God:

> 'Oh, that I knew where I might find him...
> I would lay my case before him
>   and fill my mouth with arguments.' (23.3, 4)

Encountering God in suffering

His longing comes true. After all his friends' empty theorizing, and after Job has emptied himself of his painful questionings, God does come to him: 'then the LORD answered Job out of the whirlwind' (38.1). God's whirlwind blasts away all the old arguments, and scatters to the four winds the whole system of rewards and punishments so tenaciously defended by the 'friends'. It is time now for God to question Job:

> 'Where were you when I laid the foundation of the
>> earth?
> ...Have you entered into the springs of the sea,
>> or walked in the recesses of the deep?
> Have the gates of death been revealed to you,
>> or have you seen the gates of deep darkness?'
>> (38.4a, 16, 17)

In breathtaking poetry, God is depicted as the fountain and source of all life, the Lord of creation, all-powerful and all-present. God does not give Job any neat solution to his dilemma; rather he gives him a vision of his glory and a glimpse of his mystery. Job can only respond:

> 'I know that thou canst do all things,
>> and that no purpose of thine can be thwarted...
> I had heard of thee by the hearing of the ear,
>> but now my eye sees thee.' (42.2, 5)

God comes to Job in the midst of his suffering. Job's questioning spirit has made it possible for him to encounter God, even in the centre of his agony. Formerly, Job's relationship with God had been formal and ritual. Now, his very suffering has brought him face to face with God. He does not find the answers to his questions, but he does discover that God is bigger than all our categories of him, bigger than all our theories about him – at once, a perplexing and intoxicating mystery who will not let us go. Job recognizes that this God holds all life in his hands, and he alone knows the secrets of life and death.

The drama of the book of Job ends with God saying to Eliphaz:

'My wrath is kindled against you and against your two friends; for you have not spoken of me what is right, as my servant Job has.' (42.7)

Their theorizing about God proved to be false – but Job with his agonized questioning and protest was acceptable to God. God allowed Job to throw at him his deepest hurts and grievances. Job emerges as the person of faith, the one who could be utterly frank with God, the one who would not give up believing. God restores Job's fortunes: 'And the LORD blessed the latter days of Job more than his beginning' (42.12). But was there not strange blessing in the suffering itself, the opportunity to be truly honest with God, and to discover him face to face?

Towards a spirituality in the face of loss

Our challenge is to develop a spirituality which starts to make sense of suffering and loss. What difference does the Christian gospel make to our search for meaning? How can the Christian vision of the incarnation of God in Christ lead us to some answers? What does the Cross, central to the Christian faith, have to say to us? A poor, wounded man of the twelfth century can help us in our struggle. His name is Francis of Assisi.

Bonaventure wrote of him: 'To the friars, he seemed like a second Job; the vigour of his mind increased as his body became weaker'.[1] Another eyewitness speaks of Francis' and Job's solidarity with those who suffer: 'It can be said and written of blessed Francis what is said and read of Job: "Have I ever seen a wretch in need of clothing, or a beggar going naked?" (Job 31.18)'.[2] Like Job, Francis experienced bitter deprivation. But unlike

him, he had the Christian gospel to give him some clues
to make sense of it.

Like Job, Francis was born into a household
overflowing with the trappings of worldly success. His
father was a rich cloth merchant, and fully expected
Francis to share in the fruits of his prosperity, and follow
the same career in commerce. This Francis began to do,
but the experience of illness prepared him for a
completely new perspective on life. Bonaventure tells us:

> As yet, however, Francis had no idea of God's plan for
> him. He was completely taken up with the affairs of
> his father's business and his mind was intent on the
> things of earth... Adversity is one of the best means
> of sharpening a person's spiritual perception... God
> brought him low with a prolonged illness, in order to
> prepare his soul to receive the Holy Spirit.[3]

Francis' conversion began with an encounter with
Christ on the cross. Entering the half-ruined church of
San Damiano, his eyes were immediately drawn to the
figure of Christ crucified above the altar. Francis became
transfixed with a sense of wonder and astonishment that
God should share our human pains in this way. He felt
Christ speaking to him from the cross, calling him to
'rebuild my church'. This was not a call to repair the
broken building of San Damiano, but to call the Church
away from worldly success to true gospel values. Carlo
Carretto puts Francis' response like this:

> I must confess that in that moment I was thunderstruck
> at the mystery of Christ's incarnation... the idea of
> God's incarnation that became the only answer to all the
> self-questionings hitherto in my life. Jesus was the
> epitome of all: in him heaven and earth resolved all their
> contradictions in one stupendous, vital act of divine

unity, satisfying every human thirst. Jesus' cross was
humanity's happiness, love's answer to all the questions,
the resolution of every conflict, the overcoming of every
tension, God's victory over death.[4]

What was it about the cross that so transfixed
Francis? He glimpsed that God himself comes to share
and transfigure our pain. God is not immune from
suffering – he freely chooses to embrace it, and to
transform it from the *inside* – not from the outside as
some external power reaching down from the balcony of
heaven, but *as one of us.* 'Surely he has borne our griefs
and carried our sorrows' (Isaiah 53.4). Francis put this
later in his own words:

> Our Lord Jesus Christ is the glorious Word of the
> Father, so holy and exalted, whose coming the Father
> made known by St Gabriel the Archangel to the
> glorious and blessed Virgin Mary, in whose womb he
> took on our weak human nature... And it was the
> Father's will that his blessed and glorious Son, whom
> he gave to us and who was born for our sake, should
> offer himself by his own blood as a sacrifice and victim
> on the altar of the cross; and this, not for himself,
> through whom all things were made (Jn. 1.3) but for
> our sins, leaving us an example that we may follow in
> his steps (1 Pet. 2.21)... how peaceful, delightful,
> loveable and desirable above all things it is to have a
> Brother like this, who laid down his life for his sheep
> (Jn. 10.15).[5]

Francis' whole attitude to illness was to be turned
upside down by a chance encounter with a leper on the
road outside Assisi. Normally, he recoiled at the sight of
the disfigured and disabled sufferers. In fact, he had an
absolute horror of them and would avoid going near

their colonies at all costs. But something stirred within his heart when he met this tortured man in the lane, with bandaged hands and dressed in rags. He felt impelled, constrained by something within, not only to approach the man, but to touch him tenderly, to embrace him. Later he wondered if he had not met Christ himself in this encounter. Poignantly, in his own words, Francis describes this as a turning point in his life:

> This is how God inspired me, Brother Francis, to embark upon a life of penance. When I was in sin, the sight of lepers nauseated me beyond measure; but then God himself led me into their company, and I had pity on them. When I had once become acquainted with them, what had previously nauseated me became a source of spiritual and physical consolation for me.

And in the same breath he went on: 'we bless you, because by your holy cross you have redeemed the world.'[6]

God speaks to us in pain

Francis saw a connection between present human suffering and the cross of Jesus Christ on Calvary. He saw God sharing and redeeming – literally 'buying back' or 'taking ownership of' – our pains. Revulsion at suffering turned to compassion in the literal meaning of that word – as Francis learned to *suffer with* those who were hurting. Francis too, woke up to the idea that God is speaking to us in suffering, calling us to face up to the most important things in life. C. S. Lewis put it powerfully last century:

> God whispers to us in our pleasures, speaks to us in our conscience, but shouts to us in our pains: it is his

megaphone to rouse a deaf world ... No doubt Pain as God's megaphone is a terrible instrument; it may lead to final and unrepented rebellion. But it gives the only opportunity the bad man can have for amendment. It removes the veil; it plants the flag of truth within the fortress of a rebel soul.[7]

Lewis suggests that the experience of pain can shatter the illusion that all is well with us, destroying the false idea that we can get very nicely by without God. Pain shatters the illusion of self-sufficiency, for it causes us to reach out to God either in petition or complaint. It makes us wake up to the big questions of God and evil, and can draw us into a new surrender to God, the communion for which we were created. Francis, of course, would not put it in these terms, but he came to see in every suffering person a glimpse of Jesus Christ. Francis believed that suffering does indeed have a revelatory character, for those with eyes to see it. For Francis God speaks most powerfully through the experience of poverty and pain, calling us to simplicity and trust. For him, though he delighted in the wonders of creation, God's love was revealed most clearly in the passion of Jesus. He came to see the cross, an instrument of torture, as a symbol of hope: 'by his wounds you have been healed' (1 Peter 2.24). From this self-same cross flows forgiveness and grace which can change our attitudes to pain profoundly.

Francis' whole life was marked by the experience of suffering, hardship and debilitating illness. He looked on these experiences as a way of uniting himself with Jesus Christ, whom he understood as God's love and compassion incarnate. He accepted that his vocation was to walk in the steps of the Crucified One, and to reveal to others the power of the cross. Francis reminds us that we cannot choose what happens to us in life, but we can choose how we are to respond to it. The experience of loss or suffering can be resented and faced with bitterness. Or it can be accepted as part and parcel of living on this earth as 'aliens and exiles' (1 Peter 2.11). It can even be embraced in a spirit of hopefulness as a bridge that can take us closer to God. God himself enables this attitude of openness, this ability to receive from the experience of suffering something positive. Brother Thomas of Celano, Francis' first biographer, describes how he was graced to see pain in such a light: 'Since Francis was thus worn out in every part by sufferings, it is surprising that his strength was sufficient to bear them. But he looked upon these trials not under the name of sufferings but of sisters...I think the best way to understand his suffering is this, that, as he said of others, in bearing them *there is a great reward*.'[8]

It was in solitude on Mount Verna, praying for the grace to feel in his heart the intense love enkindled in Christ, that Francis received the gift of the stigmata, receiving in his feet and hands, and in his side, an impression of the five wounds of the crucified Christ. This was the culmination of a life dedicated to penetrating the mystery of the cross. For him the words came literally true: 'I have been crucified with Christ; it is no longer I who live, but Christ who lives in me; and the life I now live in the flesh I live by faith in the Son of God, who loved me and gave himself for me' (Galatians 2.20). Carretto puts it: 'When I realized that I had holes in my hands and feet, and especially that I had a wound in my side, I understood what it meant to love without trifling. Love is indeed a serious thing, a terrible challenge.'[9] Francis realized in that moment that the Christian is invited to be fired, energized, empowered, transfigured, healed by such love.

Two years later Francis embraced death joyfully and hopefully; he called it 'the gateway of life'. He was an

Easter person, not only filled with wonder at the crucifixion of Christ but also delighting in the resurrection. As he lay dying, Francis requested that the story of Christ's passover from death to life be read, from the account beginning at John 13. Francis was ready to greet 'Sister Death' as a friend to be welcomed, not as an enemy to be feared. Brother Elias questioned how he could be so confident in the face of death. He replied, 'Brother, let me rejoice in the Lord... by the grace of the Holy Spirit I am so closely united to my Lord, that, through his goodness, I can indeed rejoice in the Most High himself.'[10] The key to Francis' hope, then, lay in his unshakeable experience of being united to Jesus Christ.

And so Francis points us to a spirituality in the midst of suffering that comes face to face with the paradox and the power of the cross and the mystery of the resurrection. He teaches us that God speaks most powerfully to us through the experience of weakness. He teaches us that the path to wholeness is through brokenness – there is no other way. He also reminds us that the path to compassion is the way of vulnerability, fragility. We do not minister to others from a position of strength, but from our own weakness. As Christ promises: 'My grace is sufficient for you, for my power is made perfect in weakness' (2 Corinthians 12.9). The paradox of suffering is the paradox of the cross, which confounds human reasoning and logic. Once again, it is the upside-down gospel which tells us that 'whoever would save his life will lose it; and whoever loses his life for my sake and the gospel's will save it' (Mark 8.35).

The power of praise

Finally, let us recall that, like Job, Francis found it possible to praise God in the very midst of suffering.

Francis is most remembered for his beautiful 'Canticle of the Sun' which celebrates God's goodness in creation, popularized in the hymn 'All Creatures of my God and King'. How did this come to be composed? An early eye-witness account explains:

> One night, as he was thinking of all the tribulations he was enduring, he felt sorry for himself and said interiorly: 'Lord, help me in my infirmities so that I may have the strength to bear them patiently!' And suddenly he heard a voice in spirit: '... be glad and joyful in the midst of your infirmities and tribulations: as of now, live in peace as if you were already sharing my kingdom.' The next morning on rising, he said to his companions: '... I should, therefore, be full of joy in my infirmities and tribulations, seek my consolation in the Lord, and give thanks to God the Father, to his only Son our Lord Jesus Christ, and to the Holy Spirit. In fact, God has given me such a grace and blessing that he has condescended in his mercy to assure me, his poor and unworthy servant, still living on this earth, that I would share his kingdom. Therefore, for his glory, for my consolation, and the edification of my neighbour, I wish to compose a new "Praises of the Lord", for his creatures. These creatures minister to our needs every day... Every day we fail to appreciate so great a blessing by not praising as we should the Creator and dispenser of all these gifts.'[11]

Francis, struggling to keep on going, and tempted to self-pity, had his eyes opened to two realities. First, he realized afresh that he was loved and cherished by God, and that he was already an heir to God's kingdom. This was a moment of reassurance for him, as he discovered the great truth that even in the midst of suffering, he belonged to God and the promise of eternal life was his. Second, he awakened to the reality of God's providence in the world, so easily taken for granted. He did more than count his blessings – he realized the abundance of God's provisions in the world, and reached out to the creatures as his brothers and sisters. This helped him to see his own plight in a new perspective, and set in the larger context of God's unfailing love. Francis discovered the grace which Paul commended when he wrote: 'Rejoice always, pray constantly, give thanks in all circumstances; for this is the will of God in Christ Jesus for you' (1 Thessalonians 5.16–18). Praise transformed his outlook, took him out of himself, and lifted his heart to God:

> Most High, Almighty, good Lord,
> Thine be the praise, the glory, the honour,
> And all blessing...
> Praise to Thee, my Lord, for all Thy creatures,
> Brother Sun... for Sister Moon... for Brother
> Wind...
> for Sister Water... for Brother Fire... for our sister
> Mother Earth...
> Praise to Thee, my Lord, for those who pardon one
> another
> For love of Thee, and endure
> Sickness and tribulation.
> Blessed are they who shall endure it in peace,
> For they shall be crowned by Thee,
> O Most High.[12]

Questions for Discussion or Reflection

1. How far can you identify with Job in his struggle with God? What questions or feelings about suffering would you throw at God?

2. Is Francis' outlook only for saints, or can it become part of our perspective?
3. What do you see when you visit someone in hospital who is seriously ill?

Prayer Exercise

Either

Spend some time interceding for those who suffer, in the manner of St Francis. He prayed stretching out his arms wide in the shape of the cross. As you do this, feel Christ enfolding and embracing all who are hurting. Close by giving thanks in the words of the *Canticle of the Sun*.

Or

Place a large cross or crucifix on the floor or low table. Take a flower or bud and hold it in your hand. See it as representing both our frailty and beauty. Let it stand for some particular situation in your own life or in the life of others that concerns you deeply. Place it silently upon the cross or upon the figure of the Crucified in a gesture of surrendering the situation to Christ who suffers and hopes in the lives of his little ones. End by reading Philippians 2.1–11.

Notes

1. Habig, M. A. (ed.), *St Francis of Assisi: Writings and Early Biographies: Omnibus of the Sources for the Life of St Francis*. SPCK, London, 1979, p. 738.
2. Habig, p. 1034.
3. Habig, p. 636.
4. Carretto, C., *I, Francis*. Fount, London, 1982, p. 33.
5. Habig, pp. 93, 96.

6. Habig, p. 67.
7. Lewis, C. S., *The Problem of Pain*. Fontana, London, 1976, pp. 81, 83.
8. Habig, p. 532.
9. Carretto, p. 130.
10. Habig, p. 1041.
11. Habig, pp. 1020–21.
12. Habig, p. 1259.

For Further Reading

Thomason, B., *God on Trial: The Book of Job & Human Suffering*. Liturgical Press, Minnesota, 1997.

Chapter 6

Struggling with vocation

The struggle to discover one's true vocation is a central and often perplexing concern of our life. We encounter many difficult questions. How can I discover God's will for my life? How can I accept a vocation that isn't exactly my first choice? How can I respond when I sense God is calling me to change direction? Can I expect my vocation to change and evolve?

In recent years, Christians have rediscovered the inspiration that the person of Mary can give. She has been newly appreciated as a figure and representative of the Christian life. Indeed, Mary can be seen as the first Christian disciple, symbolizing the vocation of every Christian: to respond to God's call, to bear Christ within and to share him with others. But little attention has been given to Mary's struggles, her wrestling with God throughout her life. As we look at these, we can find out what Mary has to teach us, both about our general role as Christ-bearers today, and about our particular vocation to do this within the unique context of our own lives.

At the event we call the Annunciation, Mary, a teenager of perhaps fifteen years, is invited to take part in God's plan for the world. She is greeted by God's messenger Gabriel with the words: 'Rejoice, O full of grace, the Lord is with you.' Mary is not only surprised at these words (Luke 1.29) but she is disturbed, troubled, perturbed – the Greek means 'thrown into great confusion, confounded'. She tries to work out what has actually been said to her. Gabriel tells her not to be afraid

– so what fears are rising in her heart? What anxieties are surfacing as she senses that God is calling her to something new?

Perhaps she is overwhelmed by a sense of utter unworthiness – 'Why me? What part can an uneducated young woman from an insignificant village possibly have to play in God's plans?' Coupled with this is a sense of deep inadequacy, a feeling that she is not qualified or talented enough for what is to come. Such fears certainly rise in our hearts when we are faced with a new challenge. We allow ourselves to entertain a fear of failure. We ask: What if I let other people down? What if I do not measure up to their expectations? Most of all, we fear rejection. What if I make a fool of myself, and people don't appreciate me? We also face a fear of the unknown – what is God demanding of me? What risks and sacrifices lie ahead? How will it affect my family? Will I need to move house? What will I have to give up? What will I have to take on?

We can identify with Mary in her moment of hesitation and timidity as she faces up to her own fears. By her open response to God's call, revealing her anxieties to him, Mary teaches us that such fears need to be expressed in prayer. In prayer, in sharing our heart's torments and questionings with God, they can be transformed. There we will recapture the confidence of Paul: 'I am sure that he who began a good work in you will bring it to completion at the day of Jesus Christ' (Philippians 1.6). In prayer we gain the reassurance of Paul: 'He who calls you is faithful, and he will do it' (1 Thessalonians 5.24). But first, fears must be expressed and surrendered into God's hands, or else they will swamp us and paralyse us into inaction. Anxiety expends and burns up vital energy. It must be decisively given over to God. Slowly, gradually, fear turns to faith. This was Mary's experience.

But not before she brings her questionings before God. Luke's account shows us how she meets with God in all honesty, in her fragility and human weakness. God unfolds his hopes that she will take part in his awesome plan for the world, and invites her to become mother of the Messiah. Mary responds with an agonizing question which echoes and resounds across the centuries? 'How?' 'How can this be?' It is our question too, when we sense that God is prompting us, urging us, into some new task. How can we cope? How will we manage? How will it all work out? How will we possibly be able to meet the challenges ahead?

If Mary's question is our question, the answer given to Mary is offered to us too: 'The Holy Spirit will come upon you, and the power of the Most High will overshadow you...For with God nothing will be impossible' (Luke 1.35, 37). Mary is invited to drink deep of the living waters of the Holy Spirit. She is promised that the divine Spirit will energize, fortify and sustain her. She is reassured that seeming impossibilities will be transformed into God's opportunities. With this encouragement, all resistance and hesitation in Mary begin to melt away. She starts to relax. She has stumbled on the very heart of the gospel, the secret of the Christian life.

The Christian faith is not supposed to be a DIY religion. We are not meant to struggle on alone, in our own efforts. We are called, rather, to surrender ourselves to God and permit him to work in our lives. The Christian vocation is a partnership with God. As we discovered in Ruth's experience, we are invited to be co-workers with God himself. Until we wake up to the reality of the Holy Spirit overshadowing us, we will never make sense of our vocation. Until we dare to open ourselves, with the vulnerability of Mary, to the Holy Spirit, the secret of the Christian life will pass us by.

The promise made to Mary is repeated to disciples in every generation, for it is the promise of the Risen Christ to the Church: 'You shall receive power when the Holy Spirit has come upon you' (Acts 1.8). Paul, too, is emphatic, crying out: 'Wake up! Don't you realize?' He stirs the Corinthians with the words: 'Do you not know that you are God's temple and that God's Spirit dwells in you?' (1 Corinthians 3.16). We need to move beyond academic assent to this proposition and actually experience it – and, like Mary, grow in our awareness and consciousness that God is not only 'out there' but actually 'within'. We need, like Mary, to thirst for the Spirit instead of craving for success, to long for the Spirit in place of succumbing to anxiety. We need to glimpse God's own longing to give us the Spirit, and to remind ourselves of Christ's words: 'If you then, who are evil, know how to give good gifts to your children, how much more will the heavenly Father give the Holy Spirit to those who ask him?' (Luke 11.13).

Through her struggle at the Annunciation, Mary gives us a vision of how things can be when we allow God to work on the raw material of human lives and when we release ourselves from the prisons and limitations of our own making. She shows us that it is possible to break free from the straitjackets we create by entertaining fears and persisting in narrow views of what God can do. She reminds us of the supreme Christian vocation – to be a channel, a vehicle, an instrument of God's Holy Spirit in the world. The dawning realization that the Holy Spirit will overshadow her, gives Mary the courage and big-heartedness to say 'Yes' to God. The promise of the Spirit moves Mary on from fear to trust, and to a point where she can surrender herself totally and without reserve to God. It is still an enormous risk, a gamble, a leap of faith. That is the character of faith – to be able to step out into the unknown and say with Mary: 'I am the handmaid of the Lord; let it be to me according to your word' (Luke 1.38).

Puzzlement and prayer

The story of Mary in the Bible can be read as an ongoing struggle to understand God's purposes, and a struggle to come to terms with what is happening to her. Luke, who takes care to give an accurate and historical account in his Gospel (see Luke 1.1–4), is particularly revealing about Mary's own inner attitudes and reactions. Her first response is to embark on a journey of some eighty miles to her cousin Elizabeth (Luke 1.39–56). This is a journey taken in haste – Mary is anxious to share both her joys and her concerns with a confidante. She does not keep them to herself, she does not brood over her confusions in isolation, and she does not procrastinate. Decisively, and with a clear sense of urgency, she speeds to Elizabeth's home to unburden herself. She knows who she can trust, and who will understand, and does not hesitate to take action. Can you imagine the encounter between Mary and Elizabeth? There were most certainly tears of joy and tears of anxiety. She sums up her feelings in the words of the Magnificat. It celebrates an 'upside-down gospel' where all normal expectations and worldly values are completely reversed. She is celebrating here the God of surprises:

> He has scattered the proud in the imagination of their
>   hearts,
> he has put down the mighty from their thrones,
> and exalted those of low degree. (Luke 1.51, 52)

As Jesus is born and shepherds kneel in adoration, reporting an apparition of angels in the sky overhead, Mary struggles to make sense of it all. She asks herself what is happening to her, and what it all really means. She is learning already to share her child with complete strangers. She is at once delighted and puzzled by what the shepherds have to say. Luke notes carefully: 'But Mary kept all these things, pondering them in her heart' (2.19). She is discovering the prayer of contemplation, in which we come before God with all our confusions and hopes and surrender ourselves totally to God. It is the experience of exposing to God the hidden depths of our hearts. It is also the experience of learning to receive from God his healing and invigorating love, which alone can make us whole.

The Greek word translated 'pondering' is rich in meaning. It denotes a 'coming together' as in a bringing together, a uniting of different rivers. Mary is reconciling in her heart different streams of thought. She is wrestling with the paradoxes thrown up by Christ, who is at once very human and yet divine, her own child yet the redeemer of the world, born not in a palace but in the poverty of a stable. The Greek verb 'pondering' can mean collecting up disparate elements, bring them into some sort of unity. It can also mean, generally, to play one's part, to contribute of one's own goods. All these meanings converge in Mary's prayer of contemplation, as she seeks to pull together conflicting forces, the desire to protect her child and the need to share him. Her hopes and her fears are beginning to meet. She is discovering the particular part God wants her to play, and is coming to terms with what she must contribute. Luke conveys to us the agonizing that Mary is facing, which develops slowly into a clearer sense of purpose, a wholeness emerging out of fragmented impressions of what is happening to her. But it is not always possible to reconcile seeming contradictions. Mary is also learning to hold the paradoxes of her vocation within a creative tension.

When forty days later, Simeon greets the Christ child
at the steps of the temple (Luke 2.25–35), she is
overcome by his joy and sense of expectancy. Luke
records: 'his mother marvelled at what was said about
him' (2.33). He repeats the same word used to describe
everyone's reaction to the shepherds (2.18) – conveying
a sense of utter astonishment, even bewilderment. Mary
is dumbfounded by it all. And then she hears the eerie
prophecy of Simeon: 'A sword will pierce through your
own soul also' (2.35). Mary is being prepared for
indescribable suffering.

Twelve years later, Mary finds herself once again at
the temple courts. After completing a family pilgrimage
to Jerusalem, Mary leaves the city without her son. She
simply presumes, takes it for granted, that Jesus will
return home with the rest of the party. It is to be a rude
awakening for Mary, a hard lesson to learn. She is
wrong. Things are changing now. Jesus is different now,
he is no longer her little boy – he has come of age. Luke
reports: 'When they saw him they were astonished'
(2.48). Luke's Greek word conveys the sense of being
absolutely astounded, even panic-struck, frightened out
of one's senses. Jesus explains: 'Did you not know that I
must be in my Father's house?' Luke puts it bluntly:
'They did not understand' (2.49, 50).

Here Luke reveals something of the inner turmoil and
confusion of Mary. She is learning that she must let go
of her son. She is learning that he has a mission – to be
about his divine Father's business. But she is also
discovering that her own vocation must evolve. She is no
longer parent to a small child; her role is changing. The
nurturing and protecting is over, and her job will be
different. She does not immediately understand. This is
a painful time of transition for her. But Luke suggests to
us how it is that Mary comes to understand what is
happening to her: 'His mother kept all these things in

her heart' (2.51). Luke's word 'kept' is best translated 'treasured up' for it means 'to watch closely, to keep safe'. She guards these events and impressions in her heart – in the deepest place of her being – the place where she can receive God's peace. She again rediscovers the prayer of contemplation as a place where we come to live with the paradoxes and dilemmas of our life.

When things happen to us that are outside our control, when there is a need to let go of something or someone we are deeply attached to, we need to learn with Mary to convert anxiety into prayer. It is there that we catch a glimpse of the divine perspective and rediscover the divine empowering of the Holy Spirit. It is in prayer that we sense that God is nudging us on to the next stage of our life's vocation. Sometimes, like Mary, we will realize that our calling must undergo a metamorphosis. Our role may be changing, and relationships and expectations need adjusting. This entails inner struggle as we learn with Mary to grieve for the passing of old ways, and discover the courage to embrace the new.

Continuity and change

If the episode at the temple was a steep learning curve for Mary, the wedding at Cana confirmed to her that her vocation was taking a decisive new direction. Mary is invited to the wedding and is alert to the needs of the moment. She initiates Christ's ministry by pointing him to the thirst of God's people: 'They have no wine' (John 2.3). The words that Jesus uses in response are literally 'What to me and to thee?' As Max Thurian explains: 'This very Semitic idiom expresses the relationship of these two human beings, in union or in opposition. In this particular case, and having been given the context, the expression should be translated thus: "What is our

relation, between me and thee, Woman?"'[1] Jesus is
indicating that the relationship is changing, and that
Mary, now aged about forty-five, must come to terms
with a vocation that is evolving and taking on a new
dimension. Vocation is not to remain static, stuck in
rigid routines and attitudes – it grows, matures, and may
take new forms and expressions. To all at mid-life,
Christ addresses these words: 'What is happening
between us? What is now going on between you and
me?' And Christ beckons us onwards, and urges us to
keep moving in the living out of the Christian vocation.

Mary's emerging role is indicated in the way Christ
addresses her not as 'Mother' but as 'Woman'. He is
giving her a new title which clearly recalls the archetypal
'Woman' of Genesis (Genesis 3.15) – Christ is calling her
to be in some sense a new 'Eve'. Mary's responsibility
and function is no longer limited to the care of the
individual Christ – it is becoming something different –
she is becoming a symbol and model of the Church, the
people of the new creation. She will accompany Jesus at
times through his three years' ministry, and walk with
him from Cana to Capernaum on the Sea of Galilee
(John 2.12). However, she finds herself in relation not so
much to Jesus as to the newly forming Christian
community – as example, carer and intercessor. Jesus
will refer to her during his teaching as one who inspires
us to hear the Word of God and do it (see Matthew
12.46–50; Luke 11.27, 28). In these words, she is
suggested as a model of discipleship, and Christ tells us
that we can in our turn become mothers to him when we
do God's will.

For her part, Mary has to grow into this new role. The
same Spirit who overshadowed her at the beginning, still
empowers her and enables her to adapt to a changing
situation. She has to break free from the limitations and
boundaries that defined her earlier role as mother to the

growing Jesus. She has to discover the resources that will allow her to take on a very different task. If her first role was the awesome responsibility of bringing Christ into the world, her new role is no less demanding and will stretch her to the utmost. But it is a painful transition. Mary has to leave behind the securities of the past, symbolized in the family home of Nazareth, and take to the road as a pilgrim. She must allow herself time to grieve for what is passing from her. It is a bereavement and cannot be rushed. Yet at the same time she is invited to step out into the future. As Rolheiser puts it,[2] we can experience 'deaths' or separations in one of two ways. We can treat something as a 'terminal death', a death that ends life and ends possibilities, a bleak finality. Or we can experience a separation as a 'paschal death', which while marking the end of one pattern of living, opens us to new and potentially richer ways of life. Christ beckons her forwards into new forms of service, calling out from her depths new or latent gifts.

At Cana, Jesus had pointed Mary towards the significance of his 'hour' (John 2.4) – the decisive hour of his passion when the prince of this world would be thrown down (John 12.27–33). It is precisely at this hour of suffering and glory that Mary is entrusted with the next stage of her ministry among God's people. Hanging on the cross, Jesus again calls her 'Woman', and says to the Christian community, represented in the symbolic figure of the beloved disciple, 'Behold, your mother!'(John 19.27). Mary finds herself once again mother, called to nurture and support not the infant body of Christ but the corporate Body of Christ, the Church.

Mary, moving now into her fifties, is depicted in this wider role in the opening chapter of the Acts of the Apostles. St Luke, who had given us such a vivid portrayal of Mary in his Gospel, now makes it clear that she has a continuing job to do as she stands among the disciples in the upper room in Jerusalem awaiting the Spirit of Pentecost promised by Christ: 'All these with one accord devoted themselves to prayer, together with... Mary the mother of Jesus' (Acts 1.14). Mary now moves into a leadership role and into a role of giving encouragement in the infant church. She who first encountered the power of the Holy Spirit over-shadowing her at Nazareth, now teaches the disciples to open themselves to his energy and guidance. We see her sharing her experience of the Spirit and urging the disciples not to lose heart but persist in expectant prayer for the promised Spirit. In the upper room Mary fully accepts responsibility for her new role as leader and carer among God's people.

In Mary we see how God continues to guide our life into new directions. Mary teaches us to remain vigilant and responsive to God's call through changing situations. She urges us to stay alert to God's nudging through successive years, as we grow older. She reminds us that vocation evolves and changes, and that we need big-heartedness and flexibility to adapt to new dimensions of our calling as they become apparent. She embodies the struggle that we too are invited to embrace – the ending of one set of responsibilities and the humble acceptance of a new, unsuspected and unsought for role. Above all, Mary teaches us that we must keep moving in the Christian life, and not allow ourselves to become fixated at any stage of our spiritual development. We must keep our eyes on the ball, spotting where God is opening up new opportunities, grieving for what must pass, and move on. She urges us to develop that most basic and essential requirement – a sense of faith and trust in God who is the alpha and the omega, who alone can see the end from the beginning. She beseeches us to stay open to the overshadowing Spirit who alone enables us to take risks, to take the leaps of faith that catapult us to the new stage of our ministry.

In the image of Mary standing at the foot of the cross, we are given a glimpse of the enormous courage we will need to face the personal costs our vocation may entail. In the image of Mary standing among the disciples in the upper room of Pentecost, we are given the reassurance that God's Spirit will enable us not only to survive but to triumph – the Spirit who is both the catalyst and inner dynamic of the Christian life.

Where can we look to find clues that will help us shape a spirituality that inspires a dynamic view of the Christian vocation, filled with the Spirit? We can turn to Gregory of Nyssa, one of the outstanding theologians of the eastern Church, who lived in Cappadocia in the fourth century. He communicated an exciting vision of the Christian life as continually evolving and progressing, energized by the Holy Spirit. His key text was the resolve of Paul: 'Forgetting what lies behind and straining forward to what lies ahead, I press on toward the goal for the prize of the upward call of God in Christ Jesus' (Philippians 3.13, 14). Here Paul is saying that there is no room for self-satisfaction in the Christian life. We should never stand still, but continually stretch ourselves towards the 'upward call'.

God invites us to make Christian vocation an adventure, in which we are beckoned to keep on growing. Gregory urges us to break free from any way of life that seems deterministic and predictable; to jump off the treadmill of dull routine which traps us into going round in circles. Rather he encourages us to discover our full potential in Christ: 'the finest aspect of our mutability is the possibility of growth in good... let us change in such a way that we may constantly evolve towards what is better, being transformed from glory into glory, and thus always improving and ever becoming more perfect by daily growth.'[3] For Gregory, each stage we reach in the spiritual journey is but a beginning, not an end. We can never say we have arrived. As the letter to the Hebrews puts it, let us 'lay aside every weight, and sin which clings so closely, and let us run with perseverance the race that is set before us, looking to Jesus the pioneer and perfecter of our faith' (Hebrews 12.1, 2). In Gregory's eyes, the greatest sin is that of complacency, of resting on our laurels.

In the Song of Songs, Gregory sees a powerful allegory of the relationship between God (the bridegroom) and the Christian (the bride). The bridegroom is a dynamic figure, ever in movement:

> Behold, he comes,
>   leaping upon the mountains,
>   bounding over the hills.
> My beloved is like a gazelle. (Song 2.8, 9)

What is his message to his bride as she relaxes and rests on her couch?

> My beloved speaks and says to me,
>   'Arise, my love, my fair one, and come away.' (2.10)

He repeats this call again (2.13). Gregory comments:

> For this reason the Word says once again to his awakened Bride: *Arise*; and when she has come, *Come*. For he who is rising can always rise further, and for him who runs to the Lord the open field of the divine course is never exhausted. We must therefore constantly arouse ourselves . . . for as often as He says *Arise* and *Come*, He gives us the power to rise and make progress.[4]

In this image, Gregory sees a powerful metaphor for the Christian vocation. We are not to allow ourselves to become too content with where we are spiritually. We are not to rest in our achievements in a spirit of self-congratulation. God ever calls us to the next stage of our development. Every point of arrival is to be a spring-board that catapults us into another adventure! We must keep moving.

This however requires of us great determination and resolve. We need to foster an unending sense of yearning and desire to grow in faith. For Gregory, it is a question of a partnership between human effort and divine help. It is the Holy Spirit who can transform the Christian vocation into an adventure of moving further into the mystery of God. He enables us to participate in the divine life itself, which animates, vivifies and completes human life: 'The rich and ungrudging Spirit is always flowing into those accepting grace ... for those who have taken possession of this gift sincerely, it endures as a co-worker and companion in accordance with the measure of faith.'[5] The Holy Spirit helps us reach our full potential and an ever-increasing likeness to God; as Gregory puts it, the soul is 'brought to the full flower of its beauty by the grace of the Spirit'.[6] Gregory pictures the Holy Spirit as a dove who not only broods over our life, but actually gives us wings to fly, never staying put for long upon the mountain, but ever ascending: 'the soul keeps rising higher and higher, stretching with its desire for heavenly things "to those that are before" as the Apostle tells us, and thus it will always continue to soar ever higher'.[7]

If the Christian is to be guided and directed by the Spirit, what part is there for human effort? Gregory is emphatic:

Do not acquiesce in His gifts, thinking that because of

the wealth and ungrudging grace of the Spirit nothing else is needed for perfection...It is necessary, then, never to relax the tension of toil or stand aside from the struggles at hand or turn to the past if something good has been accomplished, but to forget 'what is behind' (Phil. 3.13) and look to the future.[8]

Gregory is encouraging us to work closely with the Spirit in a synergy or close co-operation. The adventure of continual growth is, in a sense, an abiding struggle, but Gregory assures us: 'always nurtured by the grace of the Spirit and taking power from Christ, we may easily run the course of salvation, making light and pleasant the struggle...with God Himself assisting us in our eagarness'.[9]

Questions for Discussion or Reflection

1. In what ways can you identify with the transitions in Mary's vocation?
2. How do you find yourself responding to Gregory's vision of continual growth within our vocation?
3. What is holding you back or slowing you down in your spiritual journey?
4. How do you see yourself in five or ten years' time? What do you think you will be doing? What sort of person do you think you might become?

Prayer Exercise

Either

Imagine you are Elizabeth greeting Mary (Luke 1.39–45). What joys and sorrows does she share with you? What fears or hopes do you wish to confide to her? How does she affirm you and encourage you to keep moving forward within your vocation? Conclude with the words of Mary's song, the Magnificat (Luke 1.46–55).

Or

Write down on paper your hopes and fears for the future pattern of your vocation. Fold the paper and place it beneath a cross or Bible in a spirit of joyful trust and surrender. Conclude with the words from Sydney Carter's hymn:

> One more step along the world I go,
> One more step along the world I go,
> From the old things to the new
> Keep me travelling along with you:
> And it's from the old I travel to the new,
> Keep me travelling along with you.

Notes

1. Cryer, N. B. (tr.), *Max Thurian: Mary, Mother of the Lord, Figure of the Church*. Faith Press, London, 1963, p. 137.
2. Rolheiser, R., *Seeking Spirituality*. Hodder & Stoughton, London, 1998, Chapter 7.
3. Musurillo, H. (tr.), *From Glory to Glory: Texts from Gregory of Nyssa's Mystical Writings*. John Murray, London, 1962, pp. 51, 52.
4. Musurillo, p. 191.
5. Callahan, V. W. (tr.), *The Fathers of the Church: St Gregory of Nyssa: Ascetical Works*. Catholic University of America Press, Washington, 1967, p. 129.
6. Callahan, p. 130.
7. Musurillo, p. 57.
8. Callahan, pp. 141, 144.
9. Callahan, p. 151.

For Further Reading

Brown, R. E., *The Gospel According to John*. Anchor Bible Commentary, Doubleday, New York, 1966.

de Satge, J., *Mary and the Christian Gospel*. SPCK, London, 1979.

Chapter 7

Struggling with prayer

One of the most difficult areas of struggle in Christian discipleship is that of prayer. How can we pray meaningfully? How can we make space for stillness in a noisy world? How should we approach intercessory prayer? How should we respond if our prayers seem to go unanswered? How can I be sure God is listening? How can we grow through prayer? The figure of Martha in the New Testament can guide us through this minefield, for she is depicted as a person who is grappling with the very issues that lie at the heart of prayer. She has to work out her relationship with Jesus Christ. She has to learn to listen. She has to discover – the hard way, through making mistakes – how to bring petitions to Christ. It is significant that Luke's account of Martha's struggle is followed immediately in his narrative by the disciples crying out to Christ 'Lord, teach us to pray!' This is precisely Martha's dilemma.

We can identify with the person of Martha easily, for two reasons. First, she represents the ordinary man or woman trying to become a Christian disciple. There is nothing unusual or heroic about her – she is portrayed in all her earthiness and homeliness as an ordinary person trying to juggle various responsibilities and at the same time grow in her relationship with Jesus Christ. She seems to be a home-owner and to her falls the responsibility of managing a busy household which regularly receives visitors and strangers. She is a practical and down-to-earth character with no particular airs or graces!

Second, we can identify with her because she exemplifies precisely the kind of struggles that many of us are likely to encounter in when we try to pray. The two key passages about her shine light on two major aspects of the prayer experience: Luke 10 concerns what we call the prayer of meditation, while the eleventh chapter of John's Gospel concerns the prayer of intercession, praying for others.

Struggling to become a contemplative in action

We remind ourselves that Martha lived with her sister Mary and brother Lazarus at Bethany, a small village just over the brow of the Mount of Olives which overlooks Jerusalem, on the road which leads from the holy city, through the Judean wilderness, to Jericho. Jesus was en route to Jerusalem (Luke 10.51) when he stopped to rest at Martha's house. Luke tells the story powerfully, in a minimum of words:

> Now as they went on their way, he entered a village; and a woman named Martha received him into her house. And she had a sister called Mary, who sat at the Lord's feet and listened to his teaching. But Martha was distracted with much serving; and she went to him and said, 'Lord, do you not care that my sister has left me to serve alone? Tell her then to help me.' But the Lord answered her, 'Martha, Martha, you are anxious and troubled about many things; one thing is needful. Mary has chosen the good portion, which shall not be taken away from her.'
>
> (Luke 10.38–42)

Luke presents a vivid contrast between the two sisters. Mary discovers the art of listening prayer as she sits at the Lord's feet and hangs on to his every word. This is a powerful image of contemplative prayer: there is stillness, a cessation of all activity; Mary is attentive, focused, and receptive. Martha, on the other hand, is described as 'distracted' – the Greek word conveys a sense of being pulled in several different directions at once. Martha comes over as a person in turmoil, caught up into a whirlwind of frantic activity, and trapped within a stress of her own making. She is trying desperately to juggle different responsibilities, competing expectations.

Martha's first challenge is to re-order her priorities, to simplify her life, to delegate where necessary, to rediscover stillness at the heart of her activity. Christ tells her sternly that, at this precise moment, one thing alone is necessary – and everything else can wait, for Martha has the rare opportunity to sit still at the feet of Jesus and drink in his guidance and teaching. This is, right now, the 'good portion' which Mary has chosen. She had forgotten the scripture: 'Man does not live by bread alone, but... by everything that proceeds out of the mouth of the LORD' (Deuteronomy 8.3). Christ's words here echo the saying in John's gospel: 'Do not labour for the food which perishes, but for the food which endures to eternal life, which the Son of man will give to you' (John 6.27). Christ can offer Martha nourishment and sustenance which is far more important, right now, than a transitory meal. This, then, is Martha's initial challenge: so to discipline and order her life that she makes time and space for the prayer which just listens.

But there is a second profound challenge facing Martha. It is to become 'a contemplative in action', carrying into the midst of all duties a continual prayerfulness that beautifies and sanctifies all activities. After all, Martha was attending to jobs that needed to be done. The 'serving' had to be carried out at some point.

How can we restore proper value and meaning to these tasks? In many explanations of the Martha/Mary story we get the impression that while Mary chose the path of true spirituality, Martha was preoccupied with unspiritual things. We're told that while Mary was on 'a higher plane', Martha was stuck in the mundane.

The incarnation of God in Christ declares all activity, surrendered to God, to be sacred. God, by sharing a human life totally, by uniting his divinity to the humanity of our daily toil, has sanctified and made holy all human activities. God has become human flesh and blood. In his incarnation, God himself has laboured as a carpenter in a workshop, he has experienced long hours of toil and sweat, and has thereby declared all human activity to be the arena of divine grace. During the second century, this truth dawned on the Church. Irenaeus woke up to the reality that God, in Christ, has experienced all the stages of human life and sanctified each in turn. God has not only identified himself so closely with all human labour, he has also made possible for it to be filled with the divine.

The incarnation of God abolishes and destroys for ever the great divide between the sacred and the secular, between the spiritual and the material. No longer can life be divided into two compartments, the religious and the 'ordinary'. Christ has overcome this dualism which tried to declare that prayer was more important than work. One is no more holy than the other, because God gives inestimable value to all human life. All we do, if offered to God, can become God-bearing. Nazareth tells us that God is at home in the workplace.

And so, Christ naturally and spontaneously finds the divine in the human world. His parables reveal a deeply sacramental outlook. Everything – be it agriculture, the world of commerce, life in the family home – can reveal the hidden truths of the Kingdom. Christ finds the secrets of God's Kingdom revealed in the farmer working in the fields, in the relationship between fathers and sons, even in the dealings of debtors and business. Indeed, Jesus begins his ministry by announcing that God's Kingdom, the divine rule, is not to be looked for in a distant heaven or in a faraway utopia. It is 'at hand'. It is 'in your midst'. We need look nowhere else to discover the secrets of the Kingdom of God. They are all around us. This way of recognizing the world as sacrament, human life as sacrament, can revolutionize the way we see Martha's tasks, and our own responsibilities. Martha – and we too – can discover that our activities are not necessarily opposed to prayer; rather they can be as much a means to prayer as solitude and sitting at the feet of Jesus.

Martha, in her struggle to work this out, not only invites us to make proper time and space for stillness; she also summons us to learn with her the secret of becoming a contemplative in action – to discover God in the workplace, communion with God in everyday action, and to read the signs of the Kingdom in the daily parables of our life. Our relationships will become the raw material of our spirituality. As the liberation theologians Casaldaliga and Vigil put it:

> we have to read the two books: the Bible and the book of life...We have to sink ourselves in the Bible, but also in the conditions around us. We have to lend one ear to the gospel and the other to the people.[1]

Paul put it very clearly in his earliest letter: 'Rejoice always, pray constantly, give thanks in all circumstances; for this is the will of God in Christ Jesus for you' (1 Thessalonians 5.16–18).

This contemplative way of living helps us to discern the mystery of God's presence surfacing unexpectedly at any moment. We discovered this in Ruth's openness to the sacrament of the present moment, and in the Carmelites' practice of the presence of God. Martha nudges us to take this realization further, not only to saturate all tasks in a spirit of prayerfulness, but also to look for God in the dust and grime of daily labour. This calls us to develop a certain sensibility and alertness, but not in any 'religious' sense – rather an entirely natural openness to God who waits to meet us at every turn. So Martha calls us to discover, with her, a practical holiness – or what has been called a 'muddy mysticism'.[2]

Struggling with the prayer of intercession

When we turn to John's vivid account of Martha in Chapter 11 of his Gospel, we realize that we have much to learn from her intense struggle with the prayer of intercession. We discover that Martha invites us to take a completely fresh look at this type of prayer and have the courage to face head-on questions which we often suppress. What exactly are we doing when we pray for others? What should be our proper expectations? What should we feel when our prayers seem to go unanswered? How, in fact, should we approach intercessory prayer at all?

The chapter begins with Martha sending an urgent request to Jesus: 'Lord, he whom you love is ill.' This is pregnant with the hope that Jesus will leave whatever he is doing, and come and heal Martha's brother immediately. Martha is focusing on the presenting problem; she sees only illness, a brother who is sick. She acknowledges Jesus to be 'Lord', but seems closed in her thinking about what might happen. She expects, demands, a miracle of healing.

Martha experiences hurt and confusion when things do not turn out as imagined. She faces an agonizing wait as Jesus deliberately delays his coming to Bethany. Julian of Norwich writes: 'But sometimes it comes to our mind that we have prayed a long time, and still it seems to us that we do not have what we asked for. But we should not be too depressed on this account, for I am sure, according to our Lord's meaning, that either we are waiting for a better occasion, or more grace, or a better gift.'[3] Indeed, Jesus is actually motivated by love, and has a better gift in store: 'Now Jesus loved Martha and her sister and Lazarus. So when he heard that he was ill, he stayed two days longer in the place where he was' (John 11.5, 6). However, from Martha's standpoint, Jesus is being callous or inefficient, and she cannot understand why Jesus does not rush to her aid. Lazarus dies, and is laid in the tomb, but Martha sends no further requests to Jesus. For her, it has been a total failure, disaster, the end.

What are we doing when we intercede for others? Are we persuading God to act in a manner that he has thus far overlooked? Are we advising the Almighty what to do? Are we informing him of a situation he has not noticed? Martha's experience reveals four crucial truths about intercession, and opens our eyes to new possibilities.

Intercession is opening ourselves to glory

Jesus is very emphatic in his response to Martha's prayer: 'This illness is not unto death; it is for the glory of God, so that the Son of God may be glorified by means of it' (John 11.4). Again, outside Lazarus' tomb Jesus says to Martha: 'Did I not tell you that if you would believe you would see the glory of God?' (11.40). What is 'glory' in John's perspective? It is the visible radiance of the divine presence – a sign that God is powerfully at work. John introduces this key theme in his words: 'And the Word became flesh and dwelt among us, full of grace and truth; we have beheld his glory, glory as of the only Son from the Father' (John 1.14). How is this glory to be revealed? God's glory is manifested through 'signs' like the transformation that took place at Cana (John 2.11). But it is supremely and paradoxically to be revealed on the cross. While other parts of the New Testament suggest that Jesus first suffers and then receives glory in the resurrection/ ascension (Luke 24.26; Hebrews 2.9), John alone sees the crucifixion of Christ as the greatest moment of glorification. In the fourth Gospel, Christ can say of his passion: 'The hour has come for the Son of man to be glorified' (John 12.23; see also 7.39; 13.31; 17.1–5). Jesus approaches his death not as a disaster to be endured, but as a glory to be embraced, for the cross is the moment of salvation. From the cross flows forgiveness and hope – it is the greatest hour of God's revelation, the laying bare of his presence.

Martha is invited to pray, not for Lazarus' healing but for the revelation of the glory of God. Do we, like her, have in fact too low an expectation of intercession, asking for restoration of a deteriorating situation, when we could be asking for the revelation of the glory of God? Martha asked for Lazarus' healing from illness. She receives the astounding vision of Christ as the vanquisher of death, as Lazarus rises from the tomb. Moreover, she receives the salvation of the world for, in John's view, Lazarus' rising precipitates and leads directly to the crucifixion. As a result of his rising, the Jews take counsel how to put Jesus to death (John 11.45–53; see also 12.9–11).

Martha has to let go of her small and narrow expectations, and allow Christ to surprise her with the revelation of his glory, which is beyond her wildest imagination. As the Letter to the Ephesians puts it: 'Now to him who by the power at work within us is able to do far more abundantly than all that we ask or think, to him be glory in the church and in Christ Jesus to all generations, for ever and ever. Amen' (3.20, 21). Like Martha, we need to learn to give up any tiny-mindedness when it comes to intercession. We need to be open to the glory of Christ however and whenever it is to be revealed, most likely in the places and people we would least expect to find it.

Intercession leads us to new levels of faith

When Martha meets Jesus, she greets him with complaint: 'Lord, if you had been here, my brother would not have died.' She gets out of her system the negative feelings of disappointment and rage that had been brewing up during her long four-day wait for Christ. Nevertheless, she retains some confidence in Christ as a miracle-worker, saying: 'even now I know that whatever you ask from God, God will give you' (John 11.22). When Jesus promises that Lazarus will rise again, she confesses her faith in the general resurrection on the last day. She has hope in a remote event – part of traditional Jewish faith. Jesus invites her to revolutionize this hope when he says: 'I am the resurrection and the life; he who believes in me, though he die, yet shall he live' (11.25). In these words, Jesus turns upside-down the traditional faith Martha expressed. He smashes into pieces the remoteness of her hope by declaring that the eschatological, end-time 'life of the world to come' is already, right now, breaking into people's lives. He dares her to step out of her cocoon of inherited faith and make the leap of faith into this new revelation asking: 'Do you believe this?' Martha is summoned to take the risk of trusting Jesus as the one who, even now, ushers in the new age. Martha urges us to the same openness as we

make our prayers of intercession. Let us not confine God
to the narrow concepts we inherit, to our meagre hopes.
Let us dare to trust him completely and lead us to new
visions.

Intercession is discovering the God who weeps with us

Martha wished that Jesus came urgently to Bethany as a
visitor and miracle-worker. She wanted him to come in
to the situation, do the job necessary, and then return to
his ministry elsewhere. Once again, she finds herself
astounded to discover a different Jesus – a Lord who
wanted to enter into the very depths of her pain. John
tells us that Jesus deliberately waits outside the village,
wishing for a private rendezvous with the two sisters
(11.28–37). He wants to greet them as individuals and
minister to their hurts: seeing their tears 'he was deeply
moved in spirit and troubled' (11.33). The Greek
conveys a sense of Jesus experiencing an inward
groaning. John then puts it poignantly: 'Jesus wept'
(11.35). Arriving at the tomb, Jesus is 'deeply moved
again' (11.38). Jesus ministers to Martha in a way she
could never have expected. He is not the miracle-worker
who passes through and does his magic. Jesus comes to
put his arms around the sisters in compassionate love,
feeling their pain and confusion.

In the perspective of the Letter to the Hebrews, Jesus
continues this ministry of compassion today and for all
time from his place in heaven: 'For we have not a high
priest who is unable to sympathize with our weaknesses'
(4.15). Indeed, Christ in heaven is depicted as the
understanding advocate who 'always lives to make
intercession' (7.25). Christ maintains an unbreakable
solidarity with all who weep. He continues to share our
tears. This is a key element of intercession – as we share
our situation with him, inviting him to draw near, we

give him permission to enter our pain and confusion. This requires vulnerability on our part. Martha had to turn from a manipulative type of prayer ('Lord, he whom you love is ill – do something about it!') to a receptive type of prayer in which she could allow Jesus to weep beside her. In the perspective of Hebrews, we join our faltering prayers with the unceasing prayer of Christ the high priest. John, too, sees an eternal dimension to Christ's 'high priestly' prayer in Chapter 17, praying for all time not 'for these only, but also for those who are to believe in me through their word' (17.20).

Intercession invites us to surrender ourselves to God

Martha's experience at Bethany calls us to look at intercession in a new light. In this kind of prayer, we are not giving advice to God but rather surrendering to him our hopes and dreams, our best desires for others. Most of all, we are given the opportunity to offer our very selves to God as we intercede, placing our lives at God's disposal and standing ready, as members of the Body of Christ, to do what God prompts us to do. We may find ourselves, indeed, becoming part of the answer to our prayers, as we begin to listen and discern where our present duty lies. We may wake up to the fact that there is something positive we can do about the situation before us – and find ourselves becoming God's instrument of love towards the very ones we are holding in prayer. God can only work freely through lives that are yielded to him, and he longs to use members of the Body of Christ to bring the encouragement and support for which we pray.

If we ask 'how does prayer work?' we can begin to see that it starts by changing ourselves. In intercession God invites us to change our outlook and be open to new perspectives. He invites us to see the possibilities for glory instead of only illness or calamity. Like Martha, we can see things in a new light and recognize what we must do. We can detect in Martha a series of profound changes. She began in a state of anxiety for Lazarus (John 11.3) – behind her prayer we discern a sense of desperation. After a tortuous four-day wait during which her brother dies, Martha becomes filled with a spirit of complaint, with even a trace of bitterness and regret: 'Lord, if you had been here . . . ' (11.20). But Jesus leads her into a new discovery of faith and into new insight. She moves from disappointment to new confidence: 'Yes, Lord, I believe . . . ' (11.27).

Now something beautiful happens to Martha. A new calm descends on her: 'She went and called her sister Mary, saying quietly, "The Teacher is here"' (11.28). Silently, secretly, she experiences a new peacefulness and hopefulness as she seeks out Mary. There is no longer any trace of the Martha who is 'anxious and troubled about many things' (Luke 10.41). Martha is changing. She remains the ever-practical one, pointing out to Jesus before the tomb: 'Lord, by this time there will be an odour, for he has been dead four days' (11.39). But there is no evidence of the stressfulness that once characterized her. Joyfully she embraces her brother. And when John tells us about the supper she hosts for the twelve disciples, he writes simply: 'Martha served' (12.2). No longer is she 'distracted with much serving' (Luke 10.40). Now she seems to reveal a new serenity, a willingness to do what is needed while preserving a constant prayerfulness. The contrast between the two suppers could not be greater – she has moved from stressful anxiety in Luke 10 to a calm purposefulness.

The experience of intercession has helped to effect this change. She has allowed Christ to remould her attitudes and reshape her outlook. She has, indeed, permitted

Christ, through the prayer of intercession, to transform her perspectives totally.

Martha's struggle with intercession teaches us that this kind of prayer, far from bombarding heaven with our petitions, can become a summons to yield ourselves afresh to God, and allow him to work through us. As Evelyn Underhill put it: 'Real intercession is not merely a petition but a piece of work, involving costly self-surrender to God for the work he wants done on other souls.'[4]

Questions for Discussion or Reflection

1. How is it possible to create oases of prayer in today's stressful schedules?
2. What is your experience of maintaining a prayerfulness in the midst of activity?
3. How do you understand intercession?
4. What have you discovered from Martha's experience that rings true for you?

Prayer Exercise

Either

Prayerfully review the day that is past, asking if you have handled things and reacted in the spirit of a 'contemplative in action'.

Or

Place your needs and intercessory concerns before God in a spirit of surrender. You could do this symbolically by writing them on pieces of paper and place them, one by one, before a cross. Pray that the glory of God may be revealed in each situation. Consider, in the silence, whether God is asking you to change your attitude or do something in relation to these petitions. Conclude by using these words based on the prayer of St Teresa:

Christ has no body on earth but ours
No hands but ours
No feet but ours
Ours are the eyes through which is to look out
    Christ's compassion to the world
Ours are the feet with which he is to go about doing
    good
Ours are the hands with which he is to bless people
    now.

Notes

1. Casaldaliga, P. and Vigil, J. M., *The Spirituality of Liberation*. Burns & Oates, Tunbridge Wells, 1994, p. 107.
2. Matthews, M., *Rediscovering Holiness*. SPCK, London, 1996, p. 95.
3. Colledge, E. and Walsh, J. (trs.), *Julian of Norwich: Showings*. Paulist Press, New York, 1978, p. 251.
4. Underhill, E., *Life as Prayer (Collected Papers)*. Mowbray, London, 1946, p. 59.

For Further Reading

Ward, J. N., *The Use of Praying*. Epworth Press, London, 1979.

Chapter 8

Struggling with acceptance

One of the most unacknowledged struggles that many face today is the struggle for self-acceptance, and the struggle to be accepted by other people and by God himself. Jesus teaches us to love others as we love ourselves (Mark 12.31). But for many there is real difficulty in loving ourselves and to know deeply that we are loved unconditionally by God. In fact there are many barriers to overcome before we can both love ourselves and enter into the reality of God's love for us.

We are shaped by our past, and we can find it hard to accept ourselves as worthy of unconditional love if we have not experienced it as a child. We may persist in doubting our worth if we have only been given signs of affection when we have apparently done something to deserve it. Parents expecting too much from their child can unknowingly send out the message that it is only when he is good, when he has pleased them, that they will love him. Acceptance becomes a reward for good behaviour.

But we are shaped too by the expectations of our contemporary culture. We live in an age which can often seem dehumanizing, when we are considered as a cog in the machine, not always treated as an individual with deeply personal needs. Our society can be fiercely competitive. As adults we may be constantly seeking the approval of others, continually trying to impress others, repeatedly asking ourselves if we are 'coming across OK'. This makes us doubt our true value and worth. We can think of love as something to be earned, deserved, rather than as a gift. In the workplace there are immense pressures to perform, to impress. There is the temptation to be forever comparing ourselves with others, asking ourselves if we are as moneyed or talented as the other person. Powerful advertising encourages us to aspire to certain standards, and implies that we are not desirable as individuals until we have attained good looks, fashionable clothes and homes. This works insidiously upon our consciousness, and we can start to kid ourselves that happiness lies in matching other people's expectations. We can find ourselves wearing all kinds of masks, in the effort to achieve respect from other people.

But true happiness lies in discovering the unconditional love of God who cherishes us for who we really are. The example of Simon Peter in the New Testament can encourage us, for part of Peter's problem was a slowness to accept Christ's unconditional love. His struggle with acceptance is revealed at an early stage in the Gospels, as Jesus comes to the shores of the Sea of Galilee (Luke 5). Jesus is seeking disciples. Unlike other rabbis who looked for like-minded students to join their group, Jesus goes in search of fishermen, tax collectors and those labelled 'sinners' (Luke 5.31). He is not after the 'righteous', but ordinary men and women who know their need of God. He is prepared to welcome all whose hearts are open. And so he is drawn to the figure of Simon Peter. He is exhausted and demoralized after a fruitless night of attempted fishing, in which all his efforts were expended to no result. Jesus invites him: 'put out into the deep and let down your nets for a catch' (5.4). He calls him to leave the superficial shallows which seem to promise something but are deceptive. Peter protests: 'We toiled all night and took nothing!' But Jesus is calling him from fruitless night into a new day. The disciples haul in such a great harvest of fish that not only do the nets break but the boat itself starts to sink! What is Peter's reaction to this miracle of grace, this unexpected gift? He falls down at the knees of Jesus and cries out: 'Depart from me, for I am a sinful man, O Lord.' He believes himself to be unworthy. He does not deserve this display of Christ's power. He is preoccupied with his own sense of limitation: 'I am only a sinner – why bother with me?' He is also just a simple fisherman – surely Christ did not really want to bother with people like him? He pleads with Jesus to leave him. In his reaction, Peter reveals a deep insecurity and sense of inadequacy. He cannot bring himself to believe that he is worth Christ's attention. He feels utterly insignificant in the face of Jesus. He has, in fact, started to compare himself with Jesus, whom he has already witnessed to be a healer in his own home (Luke 4.38).

But it is precisely Simon Peter himself that Jesus has sought out. Christ has already identified his potential. He loves him. He delights in him, and he invites him to set fear aside: 'Do not be afraid' (5.10). What is the fear which threatens to cripple Peter? The fear of rejection perhaps: Simon may feel that Jesus will not want anything to do with him when he finds out what he is really like! Or maybe Peter harbours another anxiety: the fear of leaving behind his own world, in which he has established ways of coping. In his world, Peter is in charge – in charge of his home and business. It is his way of proving himself, of showing others how capable he is. Is Jesus calling him away from this? It takes vulnerability to let go of our self-defensive mechanisms, as we discovered with Ruth. We note also that Jesus says 'Do not be afraid' in response to Peter's saying 'I am a sinful man.' Perhaps Jesus is saying here 'do not be afraid of your sin. Do not worry about that now. Do not allow the awareness of your weakness to overwhelm you. We can deal with that later.' Jesus is not after perfectionism – he is after people who are ready to grow.

Clearly, Peter is astounded and awe-struck at the gracious action of Jesus. He really did not know how to respond, because it all seemed too good to be true. But Jesus has something more for him, indeed, a new vocation: 'henceforth you will be catching men' (5.10). Jesus is redirecting his life into a new purpose: bringing others into the Kingdom. With some courage, Peter follows Jesus into the future.

Discovering unconditional love

The adventure to which Jesus calls Simon Peter is a journey into the experience of unconditional love – love with no 'ifs' or 'buts', with no preconditions. This is celebrated in the scriptures by the concept of 'grace' – favour freely shown and unmerited. In the Old Testament this is communicated through the Hebrew word *hesed*, which we translate as 'loving-kindness' or 'steadfast love' (see Psalms 89, 106). It reflects the longing and ache in God's heart, his desire for each one of us. The prophets witness to this: Isaiah puts into God's mouth the words

> Can a woman forget her sucking child,
>   that she should have no compassion on the son of her
>   womb?
> Even these may forget,
>   yet I will not forget you.
> Behold, I have graven you on the palms of my hands.
>   (Isaiah 49.15, 16)

Depicting Israel as a child, Hosea puts it like this:

> Yet it was I who taught Ephraim to walk,
>   I took them up in my arms:

> ... I led them with cords of compassion,
> with the bands of love. (Hosea 11.3, 4)

This longing in the heart of God is at the centre of Christ's teaching. God's love searches us out, like the shepherd who hunts for his sheep gone astray (Luke 15.3–7). The parable of the prodigal son celebrates God's yearning for us: 'But while he [the son] was yet at a distance, his father saw him and had compassion, and ran and embraced him and kissed him.' It celebrates the dignity which God invests in each one of us: 'Bring quickly the best robe, and put it on him; and put a ring on his hand, and shoes on his feet' (Luke 15.20, 22). As Paul put it: 'he chose us in him before the foundation of the world... He destined us in love to be his sons' (Ephesians 1.4, 5). Simon encountered this love when Christ called him at the lakeside.

It was on the Sea of Galilee that Peter went on to discover Christ's love to be a transforming power, calling him beyond his limitations into personal growth. He had to learn not only that Christ accepted him for who he was, but that Christ longed to lead him forwards in a journey towards personal change and development.

The image of Peter in Matthew 14 getting out of the boat and walking on water towards Jesus is a powerful picture of Christ calling us to grow. Peter dares Jesus to invite him to climb out of the boat and onto the lake: part of him really wants to grow: 'Lord, if it is you, bid me come to you on the water' (Matthew 14.28). Jesus responds: 'Come.' He invites Peter to leave behind his personal securities symbolized by the boat – it represented his very lifestyle, and the place where he felt in charge. Jesus invites him to climb overboard – something apparently mad and dangerous! Here Peter reveals a deep struggle between longing to venture into the unknown, taking the leap of faith, and holding back. Will he look at Jesus or at the waves? Matthew tells us: 'When he saw the wind, he was afraid, and beginning to sink he cried out, "Lord, save me."' Dramatically, the narrative goes on: 'Jesus immediately reached out his hand and caught him' (14.31). The contrast is vividly set between Peter walking towards new growth and trust, and Peter sinking in fear. The image of Jesus stretching out his hand to Peter across the sea conveys again Christ's longing to lead us into the uncharted waters of total trust. Like Peter we find ourselves caught between accepting Christ's confidence in us and being a person 'of little faith'. It takes enormous determination to leave our boat and risk taking the hand of Christ, pulling us towards experiences in which we will grow and change.

When later, at Caesarea Philippi, Simon confesses his faith in Jesus, he receives an undreamed-of affirmation: 'Simon Bar-Jona...I tell you, you are Peter, and on this rock I will build my church, and the powers of death shall not prevail against it' (Matthew 16.18). Jesus recognizes in the shifting sands of Simon the potential of a rock. He sees his immense potential and latent gifts of leadership. He sees Peter's uniqueness, and the singular role he must play in the future development of the Church.

In the love and trust Jesus invests in Peter, we see the hopefulness with which Christ looks at us. He sees not 'just another sinner' but his unique creation. As John Powell tells us

> The Word of God assures us:
> ...Of course, I could have made you different: taller, shorter, born of different parents, born in a different place and into a different culture, endowed with a different set of gifts. But I didn't want a *different* you. It is *this* you that I love.[1]

Jesus accepts Peter with no conditions. He can cope with his foibles and flaws, with his impulsive character and his unpredictability. Jesus accepts and delights in Peter's individuality and his unique personality: he allows Peter to be his own man. In the wonder of the Transfiguration, when Peter babbles out the idea to build shelters – 'for he did not know what to say' (Mark 9.6) – he is not judged. Jesus understands Peter's confusion, and his struggle to understand. In Gethsemane, when Peter falls asleep at the very moment Christ needs his support, Christ again accepts him patiently. He appreciates Peter's difficulty: 'the spirit indeed is willing, but the flesh is weak' (Mark 14.38).

It is at the Last Supper that we see Peter's inner struggle dramatically revealed in the contrast between Christ's unconditional love and Peter's inability to come to terms with it. Jesus loves Peter but does Peter love himself? Can he really accept Christ's love? Jesus pours water into a basin and begins to wash the disciples' dusty feet. It is a powerful statement of his love – Jesus accepting the smell and dirt, bowing low to reveal the extent of his care. 'He came to Simon Peter; and Peter said to him, "Lord, do you wash my feet?" Jesus answered him, "What I am doing you do not know now, but afterward you will understand"' (John 13.6, 7). Peter shrinks from this: 'You shall never wash my feet.' What stops Peter from accepting this expression of Christ's love? Is it pride? Or does Peter's difficulty lie in being required to be entirely passive, to do nothing but simply receive? Peter's impulsive reaction 'Lord, not my feet only but also my hands and my head' seems to be a cover for saying that he just cannot cope with such accepting love!

To be able to receive is a great grace for it calls us to acknowledge our need, to face up to the reality that we will be incomplete without the gift that is offered. Peter's reluctance to receive the foot-washing becomes a symbol of the times we struggle to accept God's love. Our dilemma is that while we would rather be self-contained and self-sufficient, we know deep down that there is a gaping hole and void within us: our fundamental need of God. We hesitate before God because we fear that his love might change us. We need to allow ourselves, like Peter, to become vulnerable to Christ, because it is only in brokenness and real humility that we can start to experience God's love. We need to be brought to a point of brokenness, where we can honestly admit our spiritual thirst, before we can start to drink (see John 7.37). Teresa of Avila teaches us that self-knowledge is an absolute essential: 'O souls redeemed by the blood of Christ! Learn to understand yourselves!'[2]

Discovering the love that heals and empowers

Jesus is constantly desiring to lead Peter into deeper truth and to challenge narrow-mindedness. He calls Peter to expand the categories of his thinking. Peter has particular difficulty in accepting that the Messiah must suffer, and Jesus must say to him: 'Peter, you are not looking at things from God's point of view, but from man's!' (Mark 8.33, Phillips). He is very slow to accept that Christ's route to victory is through the Cross. At the arrest of Jesus, Peter lashes out and cuts off the ear of the high priest's servant. Jesus has to rebuke Peter: 'Put your sword into its sheath; shall I not drink the cup which the Father has given me?' (John 18.11). Jesus had solemnly said to Peter: 'I have prayed for you that your faith may not fail; and when you have turned again, strengthen your brethren' (Luke 22.32). Peter promises that he is ready to be taken prisoner and even die for Christ, but within hours he denies him three times. Across the courtyard of the high priest's house Jesus, under guard,

turns and looks at Peter who is hiding among the
servants. It is a look of aching love and burning
compassion. Peter leaves the palace and weeps bitterly
(Luke 22.61, 62). If this is the hour of Peter's greatest
failure, it is also a turning point in his life as he begins
to recognize at last that Christ's love for him is a
sacrificial love. He understands at last the true character
of Christ's love and the words ring in his ears: 'greater
love has no man than this, that a man lay down his life
for his friends' (John 15.13). Is Peter worth it? Jesus'
decision to embrace the cross declares that we are all
worth it.

Christ's love towards Peter and us is a healing love
that can restore us after every denial, every failure. The
risen Christ appears at the lakeside – where first he
called Peter – and asks: 'Do you love me?' (John 21.15).
The repeated question gives Peter a triple chance to
declare his love and to make good the threefold denial.
Jesus turns disaster into healing, betrayal into an
experience of growth, as he commissions Peter for new
pastoral tasks in the Church. He invites him to walk
with him into a new future, repeating the summons
heard at the very beginning: 'Follow me' (John 21.19).
This clearly relates the experience of inner healing to
discipleship.

In seeking healing we are seeking to become the
people God wants us to be. The healing ministry offered
by many churches can help us to expose our
woundedness to the risen Christ, and to express our
desire for his wholeness. We need to take the first step,
and seek out trusted friends who can pray with us,
enabling us to experience what Peter discovered: to be
gently questioned by Christ about what we really want,
to receive his forgiving and accepting embrace mediated
through the laying-on of hands, and an opportunity to
receive a new commission, and fresh affirmation. Peter's

example urges us not to avoid this encounter, but welcome it. We may, indeed, find ourselves seeking a 'healing of the memories', bringing to Christ deep wounds from the past when we were rejected and hurt. Such wounds, if they lie buried, can fester and poison our attitudes, becoming a block to self-acceptance. We may find ourselves harbouring unnecessary shame. Christ's acceptance of Peter tells us that nothing – nothing at all – is beyond his cleansing, invigorating, restoring grace.

But Jesus is not finished with Peter yet. In fact he has only just begun. Peter has struggled to accept this healing, renewing love but an even greater empowerment awaits him. In the outpouring of the Holy Spirit at Pentecost, Peter's healing and metamorphosis continues. The Holy Spirit energizes him and transforms his brokenness and timidity. Filled with the Spirit, he finds himself proclaiming the resurrection to a vast crowd (Acts 2.14) and speaking confidently to the very Sanhedrin council which has condemned Jesus. The narrative notes: 'Now when they saw the boldness of Peter and John, and perceived that they were uneducated, common men, they wondered; and they recognized that they had been with Jesus' (Acts 4.13). Bit by bit, Peter has lowered his defences and allowed the Spirit of Christ to work on him. He proclaims to others what he has discovered for himself: 'For the promise is to you and to your children and to all that are far off, every one whom the Lord our God calls to him' (Acts 2.39).

Accepting other people unconditionally

Fresh struggles await Peter. He learns very slowly that Christ's love is for every Jew and Gentile, without preconditions. The risen Christ bears with him patiently and imparts a dramatic vision to widen his horizons (Acts 10). Gradually Peter comes to realize that the new faith embraces all people, without exception. But he still allows himself to become caught up with a group of Jewish Christians who insist that any Gentile converts to Christ must undergo circumcision before being acceptable as true believers. Peter cannot quite understand that Christ's love is so radical that it overturns the requirements of the Law of Moses. Paul criticized Peter bitterly about placing this yoke over the Gentiles: 'But when Cephas came to Antioch I opposed him to his face, because he stood condemned' (Galatians 2.11). Peter is struggling to work out the implications of Christ's unconditional love which he found so difficult to accept. Finally he recognizes that Christ does not need Gentile believers to undertake Jewish rituals, as any prerequisite for full integration into the Christian community. Christ is calling Peter to reach out and embrace all kinds of people, empowered by his non-judgemental love. As Paul put it: 'Welcome one another, therefore, as Christ has welcomed you' (Romans 15.17). Yielding ourselves to Christ's love begins to transform the very way we look at others, as we learn to recognize their dignity as unique individuals cherished by God.

Our image of self

Peter's experience prompts us to search for a spirituality that will help make sense of our own struggle with self-acceptance and with the wonder of God's acceptance of us. In the writings of the fourteenth-century English mystic Julian of Norwich we discover an optimistic and encouraging approach to understanding both our self-image and our image or picture of God. Julian wrote at a bleak period of English history. The country was ravaged by the Black Death and a deeply pessimistic view of God and man prevailed. Life was short and cheap; it seemed transient and meaningless. God was feared as a stern judge angry with human sin. Julian was given a series of visions which revealed a different God: she called these 'Revelations of Divine Love'. She rediscovers the gospel of grace and hope. We are called to an eternal destiny, rejoicing in God: 'And just as we were to be without end, so we were treasured and hidden in God, known and loved from without beginning. Therefore he wants us to know that the noblest thing which he ever made is mankind.'[3] God delights in us as his highest creation: 'But because it made man's soul as beautiful, as good, as precious a creature as it could make, therefore the blessed Trinity is fully pleased without end in the creation of man's soul.'[4] We are to look at ourselves and smile! We can exult in the beauty and the dignity with which God invests us. Julian insists that God has given us great powers and a wonderful capacity to receive God himself. God's grace longs to fill and complete our individuality and personality.

And what of our failures and mistakes? Julian writes: 'He comforts readily and sweetly with his words, and says; But all will be well, and every kind of thing will be well... he does not blame me for sin. So I saw how Christ has compassion on us because of sin.'[5] She explores this insight through a parable about a master (God) and a servant (man). While about the master's business, the servant falls into a ditch and hurts himself – an image of human feebleness and failure. How is the master to react? 'And then I saw that only pain blames and punishes, and our courteous Lord comforts and succours, and always he is kindly disposed to the soul, loving and longing to bring us to his bliss.'[6] While man is tempted to be hard on himself, God takes a different approach: 'For God sees one way and man sees another

way. For it is for man meekly to accuse himself, and it is
for our Lord God's own goodness courteously to excuse
man.'[7] We need to apply to ourselves the same
acceptance which God shows to us, marked by
generosity and patience: 'And here I understood that the
lord looked on the servant with pity and not with
blame.'[8] Julian goes further: we need to fall sometimes,
for that is the way we discover the wonderful love of
God, who picks us up.

Our image of God

In reflecting on this parable, Julian came to recognize in
the person of the servant an image of Jesus. God has
become incarnate and in Jesus he fully shares our
weakness and frailty. The incarnation teaches us that
God understands us – from the inside. God comes to
earth to lead us to heaven where shame will be
transfigured into glory. 'God also showed me that sin is
no shame, but honour to man, for in this vision my
understanding was lifted up into heaven; and then there
came truly to my mind...Peter and Paul,...how they
are known, with their sins, to their honour in the
Church on earth. And it is to them no shame that they
have sinned – shame is no more in the bliss of heaven –
for there the tokens of sin are turned into honours.'[9]

Julian encourages us to rediscover the God who longs
and yearns for us, overflowing with grace. It comes to
her as a great revelation. 'Our good Lord showed me a
spiritual sight of his familiar love. I saw that he is to us
everything which is good and comforting for our help.
He is our clothing, who wraps and enfolds us for love,
embraces us and shelters us, surrounds us for his love,
which is so tender that he may never desert us.'[10] In
order to communicate this tenderness and compassion
of God, Julian boldly employs the image of Christ as

'mother'. Drawing an analogy with human parenting, she teaches that Christ cherishes us as his own beloved children, longing to protect us, nurture us and delight in us. Julian urges us to leave behind harsh images of God – like God the stern schoolmaster or God the wrathful judge.

> This fair lovely word 'mother' is so sweet and so kind in itself that it cannot truly be said of anyone or to anyone except of him and to him who is the true Mother of life and of all things... And when we fall, quickly he raises us up with his loving embrace and his gracious touch. And when we are strengthened by his sweet working, then we willingly choose him by his grace, that we shall be his servants and his lovers, constantly and forever.[11]

Julian suggests we need to unlearn some of our concepts of self and of God. We need to ponder God and man in the light of God's generosity and grace. If God is 'courteous' towards us, we need to practise a similar respect and tolerance towards ourselves and others. We need to be gentle with ourselves, and remember that God's grace respects our personality and individuality. We need to be ourselves, as God enables us to grow into the people he wants us to be, deeply loved and animated by his Spirit.

Questions for Discussion or Reflection

1. In what ways do you identify with Peter's struggle?
2. Where has your image of God, and your self-image come from? What has shaped them? Are there elements in either which need revisioning?
3. What forces today erode one's self-image? What forces can build it up?

4. What sort of people do you struggle to accept? How can Peter's experience help us to overcome prejudice or unnecessary expectations of others?

Prayer Exercise

Either

On a piece of paper, write down elements that make up your giftedness: your skills, talents, key insights. Note down also your weaknesses. Under it all write in block capitals: 'I am unique! God loves me!' Smile, give thanks, and offer yourself afresh to God for today.

Or

Get inside the story of Peter stepping out of the boat (Matthew 14.22–33). Taking the place of Peter, pray it through imaginatively. What is Christ inviting you to do? Are there any securities or attachments which Christ is calling you to leave behind? What does 'walking on water' mean to you? Is there a new challenge to which Christ is beckoning you?

Notes

1. Powell, J., *The Christian Vision: The Truth that Sets us Free*. Argus, Texas, 1984, p. 52.
2. Peers, E. A. (tr.), *Teresa of Avila: Interior Castle*. Sheed & Ward, London, 1974, p. 6.
3. Colledge, E. and Walsh, J. (trs.), *Julian of Norwich: Showings*. Paulist Press, New York, 1978, p. 284.
4. Colledge and Walsh, p. 314.
5. Colledge and Walsh, p. 149.
6. Colledge and Walsh, p. 271.
7. Colledge and Walsh, p. 281.
8. Colledge and Walsh, p. 338.
9. Colledge and Walsh, p. 154.

10. Colledge and Walsh, p. 183.
11. Colledge and Walsh, pp. 299, 300.

For Further Reading

Llewelyn, R., *With Pity Not with Blame*. Darton, Longman & Todd, London, 1982.

Pelphrey, B., *Christ our Mother: Julian of Norwich*. Darton, Longman & Todd, London, 1989.

Chapter 9

Struggling with human nature

Perhaps the most persistent struggle in the Christian's life is the ongoing battle with those sides of our character that remain self-centred; the parts of our human nature that are not fully yielded to God. The Christian wages a war against lesser motives and against the continual temptation to put ourselves first. It is easy to get discouraged when we do not achieve the standards of behaviour we aspire to. How are we to make sense of this personal grappling with sin? Perhaps the apostle Paul can help us through this.

We recall Paul as the giant of the New Testament, towering over other Christian writers with his impressive courage and theological acumen. He was indeed the founder of many churches, a powerful evangelist and missionary, undertaking vast journeys to proclaim the gospel. He was the Church's greatest apologist in the first century, and his teaching has shaped Christianity for two millennia. He woke up to the reality of Jesus Christ and sought to find the concepts which could communicate his impact on human lives. Paul is indeed an uncompromising defender of the faith and creative theologian.

In fact he is not shy in reminding his readers of his spiritual pedigree and vast achievements. In a remarkable passage he tells us of his background, his outstanding record, and his encounters with frequent dangers for the sake of the Gospel (2 Corinthians 11.21b–29). But after this impressive summary of his

Christian life, he concludes: 'If I must boast, I will boast of the things that show my weakness' (11.30). For all his untiring stamina and energy, Paul confesses his weakness.

Struggling with sin

Paul is sometimes revealing and candid in his writings. He does not conceal his torment. Frankly he writes:

> I do not understand my own actions. For I do not do what I want, but I do the very thing I hate...For I know that nothing good dwells within me...I can will what is right, but I cannot do it. For I do not do the good I want, but the evil I do not want is what I do...Wretched man that I am! (Romans 7.15–24)

William Barclay comments: 'Paul is baring his very soul; and he is telling us of an experience which is of the essence of the human situation.'[1]

We may read this account as being intensely auto-biographical, revealing Paul's own personal frustrations, yet also as typical, as Paul speaks of a condition that is common to us all. Paul confesses to being a divided self, pulled in two different directions. He describes a conflict of great intensity, between longing to live in God's way and being overcome by the rampant influence of sin. For Paul considers sin as an alien power which is trying to enslave him, and from which he desperately struggles to be free. He lives with a fundamental contradiction gnawing away at his self-confidence. Daily, hourly, he grapples with the paradox that he is a new creation in Christ yet fails to live the Christ-life consistently. How does he make sense of this? And how can we, too, come to terms with the reality that we do not live as we should?

In Paul's perspective, there are two ways of living. To describe the first, he uses the word 'flesh' (Greek: *sarx*) but he does not mean by this 'living in the body' (he has no body/soul dualism). Rather it is his chosen term to denote a way of living without Christ. The Living Bible translates this word 'the lower nature' or 'the old sinful nature', while the Jerusalem Bible calls it 'our unspiritual selves'. It stands for human nature which is not ruled by Jesus Christ but dominated by self-centred concerns. It is that part of our nature that is rebellious and contrary to God. Paul says: 'the mind that is set on the flesh is hostile to God' (Romans 8.7). He observes that this way of living is characterized by things like jealousy and selfishness (Galatians 5.19–21). It is the way we are. It is life left to its own devices. But it can become a captivity – an enslavement to the destructive power of 'sin'.

However, there is an alternative: another way of living which Jesus Christ opens up. Paul calls this 'life in the Spirit'. We can receive a 'new nature' and enter a way of living that is directed by Christ and the power of his Spirit. This is the new way of being human into which Christ came to lead us, a life characterized by 'love, joy, peace, patience, kindness, goodness, faithfulness, gentleness, self-control' (Galatians 5.22). As Paul sees it, when Jesus died on the cross, he died not as an individual person but as potentially representing the human race. His death spells the death of our old way of life: 'we know that our old self was crucified with him' (Romans 6.6). So Paul can say: 'I have been crucified with Christ; it is no longer I who live but Christ who lives in me' (Galatians 2.20). The death of Christ marks the end, the passing of the old way of living, life according to the 'flesh'. The resurrection enables a new start, a fresh beginning, a new creation, an alternative way of living: 'life in the Spirit'.

Paul teaches that we appropriate the benefits of

Christ's dying and rising through faith and baptism. This was clear in the practice of the early church, when candidates arrived at the river's edge dressed in their old clothes – representing their old way of living. These were taken off and discarded: a farewell to the 'life in the flesh'. The candidates went beneath the waters, a symbolic participation in the death and burial of Christ and a drowning of the old way of life. Rising from the waters, the candidates were robed in a new white garment representing the newness of life that Christ now makes possible – a new way of living and relating. This powerful imagery celebrates the entry into the new lifestyle that Christ enables. We are no longer 'in Adam' or 'in the flesh', but 'in Christ', 'in the Spirit'.

However, in Paul's experience, and our own, the 'old nature' – the previous set of values and attitudes – refuses to die. When Paul himself was baptized, Saul the persecutor of the Church died, and Paul the evangelist of Christ was born. But elements of our past 'nature' persist still. It does not give up that easily, and still haunts us from its watery grave. There is an ongoing struggle with the spectre of the old way of living. In fact it is like continual war: 'for the desires of the flesh are against the Spirit, and the desires of the Spirit are against the flesh; for these are opposed to each other, to prevent you from doing what you would' (Galatians 5.17). This is Paul's struggle revealed in Romans 7. Sin should be dead and buried and Christ should be ruling our lives totally. The victory is won but there are still battles to be fought. Hourly, there are decisions to be made, and the fundamental choice is this: 'To set the mind on the flesh is death, but to set the mind on the Spirit is life and peace' (Romans 8.6). So how can we live the Christ-life and say 'no' to the vestiges of the 'self-life'? How can we discover victory in this struggle with 'our lower nature'? From his own experience, Paul works out a threefold strategy.

1. Return to the waters. We must go back to the experience of baptism and remind ourselves of its truth and power. On the cross our old nature was crucified and in the waters it was drowned. Each day, each minute 'you must consider yourselves dead to sin and alive to God in Christ Jesus' (Romans 6.11). The key words are: 'consider yourselves', 'reckon yourselves'. Remember who you really are in Christ. The biblical scholar John Ziesler comments that Paul is talking about the basic 'self-understanding' of the Christian.[2] In Christ we are dead, finished with sin, unresponsive to it; we are potentially alert to God. So become what you are. Recall your new identity in Christ, your potential and your calling. Remind yourself of your new dignity. Become self-aware and stay awake. At every moment when sin tries to raise its ugly head, be decisive: 'Let not sin therefore reign in your mortal bodies... yield yourselves to God as men who have been brought from death to life' (Romans 6.12, 13). We need daily to renew our baptismal dedication to God and offer ourselves afresh to God.

This demands great determination. Paul suggests the way to do this is to visibly imagine you are casting off once more the old clothes of selfish living and re-enact your reclothing in Christ. He writes: 'Put off your old nature which belongs to your former manner of life and is corrupt through deceitful lusts, and be renewed in the spirit of your minds, and put on the new nature, created after the likeness of God in true righteousness and holiness' (Ephesians 4.22–24). In another place, Paul puts it: 'Put on then as God's chosen ones, holy and beloved, compassion, kindness, lowliness, meekness, and patience... And above all these put on love' (Colossians 3.12, 14). Or even more plainly Paul says 'put on the Lord Jesus Christ, and make no provision for the flesh, to gratify its desires' (Romans 13.14).

2. Be ready for battle. We have to strangle and kill off the old, selfish desires when they arise, for they should be dead! Paul puts it: 'Put to death therefore what is earthly in you: immorality, impurity, passion, evil desire, and covetousness, which is idolatry' (Colossians 3.5). Paul calls his readers to be ready for a fight: 'For though we live in the world we are not carrying on a worldly war, for the weapons of our warfare are not worldly but have divine power to destroy strongholds. We destroy arguments and every proud obstacle to the knowledge of God, and take every thought captive to obey Christ' (2 Corinthians 10.3–5). In another place he reflects on the type of weapons with which we should equip ourselves to face up to the negative forces he sees lying behind sin. As Phillips translates it:

> Put on God's complete armour so you can successfully resist all the devil's methods of attack. For our fight is not against any physical enemy... We are up against the unseen power that controls this dark world ... Take your stand then with truth as your belt, righteousness your breastplate, the gospel of peace firmly on your feet, salvation as your helmet and in your hand the sword of the Spirit, the Word of God. Above all be sure you take faith as your shield, for it can quench every burning missile the enemy hurls at you. Pray at all times with every kind of spiritual prayer. (Ephesians 6.11–12, 14–18)

In these words, we are reminded that we are not left to struggle on our own. An array of spiritual resources is at hand, and if we are to make any progress, we must not neglect to make use of them.

Of all the spiritual writers, perhaps it is Ignatius of Loyola who encourages us to apply Paul's teaching in a practical way. He depicts the Christian facing a daily choice between serving under the banner of Christ, with a lifestyle marked by poverty, vulnerability and humility, or serving under the standard of Satan, pursuing a life of avarice, prestige and pride. As Sheldrake puts it, this is a choice between 'Two leaders, two strategies for happiness, two views of humanity, two value systems'.[3] Ignatius, a former soldier, calls us to be resolute and strong-willed. He urges us to pray for 'an understanding of the tricks of the wicked leader, and for help to guard against them; also for an understanding of the life of truth exemplified by our true Commander-in-Chief; also for grace to imitate Him.'[4] Ignatius reminds us that we need an understanding both of the strategies of the evil one, and of the resources we have in Christ.

But a soldier needs not only weapons but training. In Christian spirituality this has been called 'ascesis' – from which we get the word 'ascetic'. It means combat or exercise. We need to build into our spirituality those disciplines which train us for the spiritual warfare and equip us with the skills we need to enjoy victory. These may include elements we have already considered: solitude, silence, meditation and frequent prayer. We may also benefit by the disciplines of regular study of scripture and discovering sources of spiritual wisdom in classical and modern writers of spirituality. The discipline of regular confession must play a regular part in our ongoing training, as we take stock of our lives, make a review of our progress and recognize by the light of the Holy Spirit any barriers to our growth. In confession we bring to God those sins and failures that we become aware of, and seek his forgiveness and grace which not only 'wipes the slate clean' but also empowers us for the next lap of the journey. After making confession and 'clearing the decks', we become more receptive to the courage and strength which the Holy Spirit longs to impart to us. We must consider, too, whether the discipline of regular fasting should play a part in our training. Paul discovered the value of fasting often (2 Corinthians 11.27). Perhaps he experienced its value in Christian prayer during his time at Antioch, where it seems a normal feature of community life (Acts 13.2). Physical hunger can intensify our hunger for God, help keep us humble, and restore a lost balance to our life.

Using the resources at hand and fine-tuning our spiritual performance through the sensible use of disciplines, we can expect little victories each day in our ongoing battle with the negative forces that assail us. Stubborn attitudes may slowly melt away. Certainly, each day we will face fresh assaults, new skirmishes with elements of 'our lower nature'. There will be defeats, when we fall down and let ourselves down, but we get up again, brush ourselves off and carry on. Paul is emphatic that final victory will be ours: 'we are more than conquerors through him who loved us. For I am sure that neither death, nor life... nor anything else in all creation, will be able to separate us from the love of God in Christ Jesus our Lord' (Romans 8.37–39). There will always be a way through this battle, because the love of God within us is far more powerful than the influence of sin.

3. Rekindle the flame. Paul knew that this struggle was common to all Christians. He wrote to a young man Timothy to hearten him: 'Fight the good fight of the faith; take hold of the eternal life to which you were called' (1 Timothy 6.12). He reminds him of the cost of discipleship: 'Take your share of suffering as a good soldier of Christ Jesus' (2 Timothy 2.3). Most importantly of all, Paul calls Timothy and his readers to rediscover the inner fire of the Holy Spirit: 'Hence I remind you to rekindle the gift of God that is within you through the laying on of my hands; for God did not give us a spirit of timidity but a Spirit of power and love and self-control' (2 Timothy 1.6, 7). To the Romans Paul pleads: 'Never flag in zeal, be aglow with the Spirit' (Romans 12.11). In likening the power of the Spirit to fire, Paul is linking in with the tradition begun with the Baptist who looked forward to the One who would baptize with the Holy Spirit and with fire (Matthew 3.11), and is echoing Luke's description of Pentecost as 'tongues as of fire' resting on the disciples (Acts 2.3). Like fire, the Holy Spirit can consume the dross and cleanse and purge us bit by bit of our imperfections. Like fire he can energize and invigorate us in the midst of struggle. And inextinguishable fire is highly contagious too!

Most of all, Paul has discovered that the Holy Spirit can bring alive into our consciousness the fundamental reality that we are sons and daughters of God, and no longer slaves to sin. 'When we cry, "Abba! Father!" it is the Spirit himself bearing witness with our spirit that we are children of God' (Romans 8.15, 16). For Paul, the secret of surviving the struggle, the key to unlocking the doorway to victory, is the rediscovery of the presence of the divine Spirit within us. We are but fragile and cracked vessels – the Spirit is the eternal abiding at the very centre of our new natures. We are weak and inconsistent – he is unchanging and gently powerful as he is given room in which to work upon us. This is Paul's testimony: 'But we have this treasure in earthen vessels, to show that the transcendent power belongs to God and not to us. We are afflicted in every way, but not crushed; perplexed, but not driven to despair' (2 Corinthians 4.7, 8). Paul's experience can be ours as we discover, with him, that the Holy Spirit can lead us into true liberty: 'where the Spirit of the Lord is, there is freedom' (2 Corinthians 3.17). We need to give the Holy Spirit the chance to work upon us, liberating us from our captivities, and transforming us into the fire-giver, Jesus Christ.

In our study, Paul emerges as a very human figure. The strong and confident exponent of the new faith reveals himself to be fragile, prone to weakness. In one place he admits to a very personal struggle which he calls 'a thorn in the flesh'. We don't know the nature of this physical or spiritual dilemma, but it is symbolic of the struggles we have been considering here. It is something that would not go away; but there was a way through the struggle: 'Three times I besought the Lord about this, that it should leave me; but he said to me, "My grace is sufficient for you, for my power is made perfect in weakness."' With Paul we too can say: 'I will all the more gladly boast of my weaknesses, that the power of Christ may rest upon me. For the sake of Christ, then, I am content with weaknesses...; for when I am weak, then I am strong' (2 Corinthians 12.8–10).

Questions for Discussion or Reflection

1. What do you make of Paul's distinction between 'the lower human nature' and 'life in the Spirit'? Does it correspond to your experience?

2. Which of Paul's three strategies for coping do you find most helpful? What ways can you commend?

Prayer Exercise

Either

Light a candle and use it as a focus for meditating on Paul's words: 'Fan into a flame the gift of God within you.' Consider how the Holy Spirit is like fire in your life – cleansing, energizing, contagious. Conclude with words from Charles Wesley's great hymn:

O Thou who camest from above,
The pure, celestial fire to impart,
Kindle a flame of sacred love
on the mean altar of my heart.

There let it for thy glory burn
with inextinguishable blaze,
and trembling to its source return
in humble prayer and fervent praise.

Or

Read Ephesians 6.10–18. Review your spiritual armoury, using this as a sort of checklist, reflecting for example on your grasp of Christian truth, your willingness to live the gospel, your readiness to ponder the Word of God, the quality of your times of prayer. Conclude by using these words adapted from the Baptismal Service:[5]

Let us not be ashamed to confess the faith of Christ crucified.
Let us fight valiantly under the banner of Christ against sin, the world and the devil, and continue his faithful soldiers and servants to the end of our lives.
May almighty God deliver us from the powers of darkness, and lead us in the light and obedience of Christ. Amen.

Notes

1. Barclay, W., *The Letter to the Romans*. Daily Study Bible, Saint Andrew Press, Edinburgh, 1990, p. 98.
2. Ziesler, J., *Paul's Letter to the Romans*. SCM Press, London, 1993, p. 162.
3. Sheldrake, P., *The Way of Ignatius Loyola: Contemporary Approaches to the Spiritual*

Exercises. SPCK, London, 1991, p. 92.

4. 'Meditation on Two Standards' in Corbishley, T., (tr.), *The Spiritual Exercises of Ignatius Loyola.* Anthony Clarke, Wheathampstead, 1973, p. 53.

5. Central Board of Finance of the Church of England, *The Alternative Service Book 1980.* Mowbray, Oxford, 1980.

For Further Reading

Foster, R., *Celebration of Discipline.* Hodder & Stoughton, London, 1980.

Sanders, E. P., *Paul.* Oxford University Press, Oxford, 1996.

Whitney, D. S., *Spiritual Disciplines for the Christian Life.* Scripture Press, Amersham, 1991.

Chapter 10

Jesus: God with us in our struggles

The Christian gospel proclaims that God is not far away, locked up in a distant heaven. He comes to be born as one of us, to share our human life completely. Indeed, in Jesus Christ he comes to open up a way through the struggles we face.

It is no accident that the Gospels begin the account of Christ's ministry with his baptism in the river Jordan. Baptism declares a washing away of sin and a readiness to repent – so why does Jesus need baptism? A dumbfounded John protests and tries to prevent him saying, 'I need to be baptized by you, and do you come to me?' (Matthew 3.14). Jesus embraced baptism to declare his radical solidarity with ordinary men and women. In submitting to baptism, he declares himself to stand among and not over against humanity in its search for God. His baptism proclaims that he is indeed Emmanuel, 'God with us' (Matthew 1.23), coming to lead us into his Kingdom from the inside of our condition, not from the outside. His baptism declares that God really has become one of us.

This is the vision of the New Testament. In the Letter to the Hebrews, the Christian life is depicted as a pilgrimage: 'For here we have no lasting city, but we seek the city which is to come' (Hebrews 13.14). In our earthly journey, we have before us a model and example: 'Let us run with perseverance the race that is set before us, looking to Jesus' (12.1, 2). But in what way are we to 'look to Jesus'? Who is Jesus for us? The writer goes on: 'looking to Jesus the pioneer and perfecter of our faith'. Hebrews calls Jesus the pioneer. The Greek word *archegos* means a trail-blazer – someone who cuts a way forward to enable others to follow. Hebrews puts it: 'For it was fitting that he, for whom and by whom all things exist, in bringing many sons to glory, should make the pioneer of their salvation perfect through suffering. For he who sanctifies and those who are sanctified have all one origin. That is why he is not ashamed to call them brethren' (2.10, 11). God has become our brother. He comes to lead us in our earthly journey. The route to glory may be a pathway of struggles, even suffering. Jesus shares our limitations – as Paul had put it, quoting an early Christian hymn: he 'emptied himself, taking the form of a servant, being born in the likeness of men' (Philippians 2.7). In the perspective of the Letter to the Hebrews, God himself, in Jesus Christ, pioneers a pathway to heaven, creating a breakthrough, a passage through our struggles, to enable us to reach our ultimate goal. The Letter has two particular struggles in view.

First, Hebrews recalls that Christ grappled with temptation and was exposed, as we are, to negative forces seeking to pull him down: 'For we have not a high priest who is unable to sympathize with our weaknesses, but one who in every respect has been tempted as we are, yet without sinning' (4.15). In his forty gruelling days in the wilderness after his baptism, Jesus came face to face with the powers of evil and entered into combat with three powerful temptations. He was urged to misuse his power ('command this stone to become bread', Luke 4.3); he was tempted to compromise his values ('worship me', 4.7); he was encouraged to sensationalize ('throw yourself down from here', 4.9). These were short cuts to recognition – the timeless temptations to power, pride and prestige. It is significant that immediately after his baptism, which proclaimed his solidarity with human lives, Jesus faced temptations which will face men and women in every age. Mark puts it vividly: 'He was with the wild beasts' (Mark 1.13) – representing the ferocious and untamed forces which threaten us. Paul is later to offer consolation: 'No temptation has overtaken you that is not common to man. God is faithful, and he will not let you be tempted beyond your strength, but with the temptation will also provide the way of escape, that you may be able to endure it' (1 Corinthians 10.13). In the perspective of Hebrews, his temptations enable Jesus to inspire and hearten Christians of every age: 'For because he himself has suffered and been tempted, he is able to help those who are tempted' (Hebrews 2.18).

Second, the author of Hebrews recalls Christ's impassioned struggles in prayer: 'In the days of his flesh, Jesus offered up prayers and supplications, with loud cries and tears' (Hebrews 5.7). Jesus cries out to God in prayer, sharing the human emotions of anguish and distress. As W. L. Lane puts it: 'The reference to "cries and tears" describes prayer in a setting of crisis.'[1] Perhaps the experience of Gethsemane is in view: where Jesus enters the darkness of agony and 'began to be greatly distressed and troubled' (Mark 14.33). In a garden Adam and Eve began their struggle with the serpent; in another garden Christ wrestles with the powers of darkness. Indeed the hour of his passion is the culmination of three years of conflict with negative forces, only overcome by the power of prayer (see Mark 9.29). In the Letter to the Hebrews, this experience of anguished prayer is a deeply learning experience for Jesus, for it goes on: 'Although he was a Son, he learned obedience through what he suffered' (5.8). As Oscar Cullmann has pointed out: 'This expression, which has never been successfully explained away, presupposes an inner human development. The life of Jesus would not be really human if its course did not manifest a *development*.[2] Jesus learns – he discovers through struggle how it is possible to know God's will and follow it through, even in the midst of suffering. And so, as D. G. Peterson puts it: 'The perfecting of Christ "through suffering" provides a pattern for Christian discipleship. Christians share to a certain extent in the same struggle or contest that Christ endured, and because he pioneered the way, they have the same prospect of enjoying his victory if they share his faith and manifest the same sort of perseverance.'[3]

Throughout his incarnate ministry, Jesus reveals himself to be vulnerable to many different kinds of struggles. He recognizes the dangers of stress and resolutely makes time and space for quiet (Luke 5.16). He experiences anger and frustration, especially with religious leaders, and gives this the fullest expression, overturning the tables in the temple forecourts (John 2.15; see also Matthew 21.12). He wrestles with issues of justice and forgiveness (John 8.1–11). He weeps at the tomb of Lazarus and enters the pain of human bereavement. He has to work out his developing vocation and self-identity in the face of opposition (see John 8).

But the Gospels also testify to the immense longing of Jesus to get alongside those who struggle. In Mark's Gospel, there is a brutal honesty about the disciples' failure to understand: 'his disciples asked him about the parable. And he said to them, "Then are you also without understanding?"' (Mark 7.17, 18; see also 6.52). Jesus deals with the disciples' slowness of response with patience and further teaching. Sometimes, it is true, he gets exasperated with them (see Mark 8.17–21), but still he bears with them. They are, after all, the people he really wanted, for he had 'called to him those whom he desired' (Mark 3.13). He had chosen them, one by one, recognizing both their unique potential and their individual foibles.

St Luke's Gospel especially underlines the theme of Christ's compassion. This is the Gospel that gives us the parable of the prodigal son and the parable of the wayward sheep (Chapter 15). This is the Gospel where we see Christ's love for such disparate individuals as the sinner-woman who washed his feet with her tears (7.36–50); the man with legions of demons (8.26–39); Zacchaeus the fraudulent tax-collector (19.2–10). Each of these strugglers Christ embraces, welcomes, restores. God in Christ comes to the confused and leads them gently into his kingdom.

The heart of the gospel is a message of 'dying – to live'. We are invited to participate in a paschal journey leading to resurrection by way of the cross. In the upper room, Jesus says to the puzzled Peter: 'where I am going you cannot follow me now; but you shall follow afterward' (John 13.36). The route to newness of life is through crucifixion. Jesus says to the multitude and to his disciples: 'If any man would come after me, let him deny himself and take up his cross and follow me. For whoever would save his life will lose it; and whoever loses his life for my sake and the gospel's will save it' (Mark 8.34, 35). Here Jesus is contrasting two opposite attitudes. 'Saving one's life' is a self-protective attitude which seems to ensure safety but in fact represents the closing-in of one's self, a sense of hoarding one's personal resources, withdrawal. 'Losing one's life' is about taking risks, becoming vulnerable, being ready for the struggle however it may manifest itself. Jesus is calling us to this latter path which, though costly, leads to salvation and wholeness, to resurrection, to God himself.

Jesus Christ is, then, the pioneer, the one who goes ahead of us, who finds the route to breakthrough in our struggles. But we also find that he is beside us at every moment. The writer to the Hebrews celebrates the astonishing fact: 'Jesus Christ is the same, yesterday, and today, and for ever' (Hebrews 13.8). As he once walked beside the disciples and supported them in their struggles, so today he offers us his hand and invites us to walk with him into the future. Indeed, we look to him our pioneer, brother and fellow-pilgrim. He opens before us a vision of life as it can be lived. So we take heart: 'Therefore lift your drooping hands and strengthen your weak knees, and make straight paths for your feet' (Hebrews 12.12).

Our journey began with Genesis. We have met characters who have struggled and found a way through. Finally, we turn to the last book of the Bible, where the Risen Christ offers many special blessings to those who overcome in their struggles. First addressed to first-century communities, these blessings answer struggles which confront Christians in every age, and offer timeless rewards depicted in richly symbolic language. The church at Ephesus struggled with the challenge of loving Christ passionately, and to them the pledge is made: 'To him who conquers, I will grant to eat of the tree of life, which is in the paradise of God' (Revelation 2.7). In these words, Jesus promises eternal life to those who overcome. The Christians at Pergamum were struggling with compromise: the temptation to water down the truth and the demands of the gospel. To them the Risen Christ makes the promise: 'To him who conquers I will give some of the hidden manna, and I will give him a white stone, with a new name written on the stone which no one knows except him who receives it' (2.17). He is promising something very personal and individual to overcomers, a fuller revelation of himself to those who do not lose the truths that they have already discovered. In the gift of the 'new name', Christ promises a new future, a new destiny.

The church at Thyatira was grappling with issues of sexuality and exploitation. But to those who seek a way through this darkness Christ promises 'the morning star' – his very self – to light up the shadows and bring reassurance (2.28). The community at Sardis was facing a paralysis, a sleep, a deep lethargy. What is Christ's promise to those who rouse themselves from this? 'He who conquers shall be clad thus in white garments' (3.5). This suggests a reinvigoration and a return to the grace first communicated in baptism. To the church at Philadelphia, Jesus says: 'I know your works. Behold, I have set before you an open door, which no one is able to shut; I know that you have but little power, and yet you have kept my word' (3.8). Christ had been trying to lead them into new opportunities for growth, but they had felt powerless. Yet he sees their potential and promises: 'He who conquers, I will make him a pillar in the temple of my God' (3.12). God can make those who feel inadequate and frail into a pillar – something solid, something dependable, something essential.

Finally, the Risen Christ addresses the church at Laodicea. They are the greatest strugglers of all, described as 'lukewarm, and neither cold nor hot' (3.16). They had lost their passion for Christ; their determination as disciples had waned. Some of them were on the point of giving up altogether. To them Christ offers a breath-taking pledge: 'Behold, I stand at the door and knock; if any one hears my voice and opens the door, I will come in to him and eat with him, and he with me' (3.20). He offers them a new chance of communion with him. He desires to get inside of them and re-energize them, if they but open the door.

To the greatest of strugglers, then and now, Christ makes this matchless promise: 'He who conquers, I will grant him to sit with me on my throne, as I myself conquered and sat down with my Father on his throne' (3.21). In these timeless words, Christ reassures us that there will be a way through our struggles, even as Christ faced his Gethsemane and Calvary and broke through to the experience of resurrection. There is a way to victory, to overcoming, to the experience of Easter. Holding fast to this eternal promise, let us embrace our struggles and discover them to be, indeed, pathways to growth and wholeness.

Notes

1. Lane, W. L., *Hebrews: A Call to Commitment.* Hendrickson, USA, 1985, p. 81.
2. Cullmann, O., *The Christology of the New Testament.* SCM Press, London, 1963, p. 97.
3. Peterson, D. G., *Hebrews and Perfection.* Cambridge University Press, Cambridge, 1982, p. 187.